Icy Sedgwick

Bring Me LOVE

Finding and Keeping Love Using Divination and Folk Magic

WATKINS
Sharing Wisdom
Since 1893

BRING ME LOVE
By Icy Sedgwick

First published in the UK and USA in 2026 by Watkins,
an imprint of Watkins Media Limited, Unit 11, Shepperton House,
83–89 Shepperton Road, London N1 3DF

enquiries@watkinspublishing.com

Editorial Director: Ella Chappell
Commissioning Editor: Fiona Robertson
Managing Editor: Brittany Willis
Editorial Assistant: Caitlin Nolan
Head of Design: Karen Smith
Typesetting: Eleri Santon
Commissioned Artwork: Becca Thorne
Production: Uzma Taj

Typeset in Cera Pro & Esmeralda
Printed and bound in China

The manufacturer's authorised representative in the EU for product safety is:
eucomply OÜ – Pärnu mnt 139b-14, 11317 Tallinn, Estonia,
hello@eucompliancepartner.com, www.eucompliancepartner.com

A CIP record for this book is available from the British Library

ISBN: 978-1-78678-974-7 (Hardback)
ISBN: 978-1-83681-020-9 (eBook)

10 9 8 7 6 5 4 3 2 1

MIX
Paper | Supporting
responsible forestry
FSC
www.fsc.org   FSC® C005748

www.watkinspublishing.com

CONTENTS

INTRODUCTION

Folklore bursts at the seams with charms and practices to help people bring more love into their lives. In fact, only money rivals love as a subject of magic and ritual (and there's nothing wrong with wanting more of either of them). While magic works actively to attract love, there is also a myriad of divinatory traditions to give people information about their love lives, from who their future partner might be to whether they will find love at all. Love magic and divination both still hold our attention here in the 21st century. At the time of writing, a Google search for the term "love divination" gives 24.9 million results, while "love magic" brings up 967 million! There are hundreds if not thousands of books and social media accounts talking about love magic, and while many of them are excellent, most of them focus on how to practice it; far fewer explore what the people of the past actually did.

This book is an introduction to the vast topic of love magic and divination. I want to show what people did in the past – and sometimes continue to do now – but also to suggest how we can use folklore as a starting point for creating our own traditions, rituals and practices. Folklore is an immense field of study, but at its heart is a focus on preserving what ordinary people did, believed or thought, and that makes it a great starting point for us. Digging into the records, which, true, can sometimes be biased by the perspectives of those who created them, grants us a window into these past practices. And we can soon see that little separates us from our forebears except time and technology.

Practices appear in the historical record in the trials of cunning folk hired to perform love magic or divination on behalf of clients, and in the trials of those who hired them. These cunning folk can best be described as "service magicians", plying their trade to help clients recover lost objects, discover thieves, treat illnesses, heal livestock, get justice in legal matters, locate riches and, yes, find partners. Make no mistake, they were not witches, but rather practitioners with particular skills that others sought for their help.

Witches, in a historical sense, were those people accused of using occult powers derived from the Devil or his minions for malevolent ends. There's no way to say if they had such powers, and many, if not most, of those accused would have been Christians who would be horrified by such accusations of witchcraft. There's a tendency on social media to assume the witches of old were all merely herbalists or people who worked with plants who fell foul of the patriarchy, but the reality is more complicated.

That's not to say there was no crossover in how the skills of cunning folk were perceived. For example, in 1444, two women from Durham found themselves accused of witchcraft after telling single women how to snare their desired husbands. Given marriage was the way by which a man secured his legacy, you can see why there was such social concern about the validity of wedlock.[1] No one wanted to feel as though they had been ensnared without their full consent.[2]

Yet even royalty was not above using love magic, or at least the public perception was that they were not. In 1469, Jacquetta, Duchess of Bedford, was accused of using witchcraft to compel Edward IV to marry her daughter, Elizabeth Woodville. The secrecy surrounding the wedding, which was hardly surprising given Edward was apparently betrothed to someone else, and Elizabeth's relatively low social status, certainly seemed to support the case for magical compulsion.

Of course, such accusations were also a relatively easy way for a vindictive rival to cast aspersions. It is possible that

the Earl of Warwick's irritation at the rapid rise of the Woodville family at the expense of his own family, the Nevilles, led him to attack Jacquetta to bring down the Woodvilles. After all, directly attacking Elizabeth herself would have been too risky, as Elizabeth was now queen. Warwick produced an unrecognizable figure made of lead as part of his accusation that Jacquetta had used image magic to force Edward to fall in love with Elizabeth (we'll explore the use of poppets further in Chapter 6). Warwick couldn't make the charges stick, however, and Parliament officially exonerated Jacquetta in 1470.

The accusation of love magic reared its ugly head again after Edward IV's death when Richard of Gloucester, Edward's younger brother, said that Elizabeth had used sorcery to ensnare the king. He hoped to have the marriage declared invalid, and thus her children disinherited, leaving him heir to the throne. It turned out that Richard needed Elizabeth at court to legitimize his rule in the face of the threat from Henry Tudor, so Elizabeth was never formally charged of witchcraft, but the accusations were never entirely dispelled. Mud sticks, after all.

I can't help thinking that if Elizabeth really had magical powers, her boys would not have ended up in the Tower of London before they disappeared into history as the famed Princes in the Tower. Still, the question of whether they were murdered, and by whom, is beyond our focus here.

Eventually, the dislike of love magic passed into law. In 1541, Henry VIII passed the Act against Conjurations, Witchcrafts, Sorcery and Enchantments, which outlawed a range of magical practices, including any which "provoke any person to unlawfull love". This didn't cover the work of cunning folk, who would help their clients find lost items, cure ailments or solve marital problems, but rather sought to outlaw magic with malicious intent. That included hiring a cunning person for their help in securing a specific love interest who had previously shown no interest in the client.

Edward VI and Elizabeth I tinkered with witchcraft legislation, and an Act against Witchcraft and Sorcerie (1586) in Ireland returned the concern with the provocation of unlawful love to the statute book. Magically forcing someone to love you was considered "unlawful love", which made practising love magic very dangerous.

Other acts came and went until the 1735 Witchcraft Act, which repealed the acts passed in England and Scotland, though the Irish Act wasn't repealed until 1821! By this point, magic, fortune telling and witchcraft were legally considered impossible. Practitioners of love magic could now be tried as a fraud, but were no longer seen as dangerous members of society and couldn't be executed for their activities.

Some accounts of love magic do exist in much older records. A medieval source explained that practitioners of love magic would work with the goddess

Venus and any spirits she controlled.[3] Naturally, there's no way of knowing if ordinary people gave praise to Venus, goddess of love, beyond the confines of ancient Rome; if they did so, then it was likely in secret. Theologians denounced handbooks that included instructions to force demons to bring beautiful women to the practitioner, among other astonishing feats. Written in the 13th century, the *Cantigas de Santa Maria* (*Canticles of Holy Mary*) feature a story in which a priest forced demons to compel a girl to love him by threatening to trap them in a bottle if they didn't help. The story explains that they succeeded in making the girl desire the priest, but the Virgin Mary intervened and not only was the girl saved, but the priest ended up in hell.[4]

The "demonic" side of love magic is a huge topic, and I feel it's more useful to focus on the potions and charms available to ordinary people, or those practices favoured by cunning folk, which were more accessible than the services of a magician. We will lightly touch on some of the sorcery used by magicians when we get to poppets, but we're going to be more concerned with ordinary people and their everyday practices in this book.

USING LOVE SPELLS

You can't have love magic without spells, so it's worth taking a quick detour into the types of love spells in the historical record. The spells that survive are the ones that were written down, meaning they appear in books created by and for men, who were much more likely to be literate than women. The charms used by cunning women, which involved everyday items and accessible practices, often don't appear unless they're mentioned in court records or were collected in the 19th century by folklorists. This naturally skews what's available, so while much of this book examines more mundane (and often benign) spells and charms, it wouldn't be complete without some acknowledgement of the darker side of love magic.

The *Picatrix*, for example, was a magical book found in libraries across Europe from the mid-fifteenth century. Aimed at male magicians with the literacy required to study the text, it naturally included a ritual for seducing women.

It directed the magician to heat some blood taken from the man for whom the spell was being performed (who could be the magician himself), before adding dried hare's blood, wolf's brain, cattle fat, amber, nutmeg and camphor. The magician would combine the ingredients before mixing the resulting concoction with wine or honey, and adding it to food. Throughout the entire process, the magician should keep the woman in question firmly in mind. Once the food was prepared, the magician would throw incense and galbanum gum into the fire and recite an incantation. Either he or his client would then ply the woman with the mixture, ensuring she ate the entire quantity. As long as it sat in her stomach, she would go wherever the man chose.[5]

Other spells were aimed at manipulating women into accepting marriage proposals. Such was the fear of magical interference in the course of true love that priests in the early 13th century might ask parishioners if they'd used magic to cajole someone into marriage.[6] Ensuring both parties legitimately consented to the marriage was a key priority.

Women might use such magic too, especially if they found themselves pregnant and doubtful their male partner would follow through on promises of marriage. The use of these spells to ensnare a spouse suggests the desire for a marriage partner was not solely restricted to women, and that men were equally capable of seeking magical assistance in finding a wife, including when they had set their heart on a woman who had no interest in marrying them.

The story of saints Cyprian and Justina is a fascinating illustration of the male desire to seek love from a woman. A man hired the pagan sorcerer Cyprian to bewitch Justina, a Christian virgin, and make her fall in love with him. Cyprian conjured demons to force Justina to love the man, but no matter what the demons did, Justina's faith remained strong. Completely amazed by her ability to fend off the demons through faith alone, Cyprian renounced his magical ways and converted to Christianity. He and Justina died as martyrs, so there is no happy ending to the story, but medieval writers used it as an example to show that being pious was enough to defend yourself against love magic.[7]

GENDER, BIAS & ETHICS

This leads us nicely to consider the idea of gender. Many accounts of folklore practices suggest they were done by women, while scholarly magical texts included practices designed to be used by men. Other texts don't specify one way or the other, and we even find rituals designed to be used by both men and women, as we shall see.

While the focus on folk love magic and divination as being practiced by mainly women might look sexist to us from a 21st-century perspective, marriage was an economic necessity for most women in earlier centuries, and not finding a partner could bring financial and social hardship. Marriage brought a degree of security, depending upon the job or income of a woman's husband, although we would be naive to assume it also brought domestic bliss.

We only need to look at the work of writer Jane Austen to see this in action in the middle and upper classes. In her classic *Pride and Prejudice* (1813), the Bennett sisters needed to make good marriages because their father's money would be inherited not by them but by their cousin, the odious Mr Collins, who was his closest male relative. While a need to marry for financial security sounds horribly pragmatic now, you will notice

how many of the rituals and divinatory practices found in folklore still focus on acquiring *love*, not just finding a random well-off person to marry.

Many of the folk practices also seem heteronormative because they reflect the cultural context in which they emerged. Where accounts of practices specify they were used by girls or women, I have indicated this in the text, but otherwise, if the folkloric record preserved the practice, but not who was intended to use it, I have tried to use gender-neutral language such as the word "partner". This also removes the pressure to find a spouse! Feel free to adapt these practices to suit your own gender expression or sexuality, as we live in our own time and cultural context.

There is also a bias in assumptions that women were more likely to offer their magical services to other women, but, as noted by folklorist and historian Owen Davies, both male and female practitioners offered a range of love charms and potions in England.

This book has a northern and western European focus as that is my cultural and ancestral background, with an eye also on the ancient world, where many of these ideas originated. (I hope that others will write similar books covering love magic and divination in other regions of the world!) Where possible, I have mentioned where the tradition was recorded, but the place of origin is not known in all cases. Some traditions vary from one place to another, so you may have heard of practices that are slightly different to the ones offered here. This demonstrates the difficulty of preserving folklore: the folklore that was recorded in writing became fixed by the folklorist, while folklore passed on orally had the opportunity to evolve. Accounts of folklore are also coloured by the bias of the collector, so we need to be mindful that the collector was often a 19th-century clergyman!

There's no way to know if any of these practices ever worked, because the collectors recorded the instructions but not their results or how many people actually used them. That said, it's likely that people had enough belief in the likelihood of success to pass them on to other love hopefuls and to the folklorists who collected them. Another issue, when it comes to the more unusual folklore, is that you can never be sure if someone simply made up a story to fool a gullible collector!

Folklore is not simply something we find in the historical record; rather, it is part of our lived experience, so if you choose to replicate one of the practices in this book, you are taking part in a long, varied and ever-changing tradition. Adapting practices for your own situation adds a new note to the symphony of folklore; throughout history, practices would have been continually adapted based on what was available in a given place and time.

Today, in many parts of the West, women no longer need to marry to gain financial security (though singles everywhere will understand the cost of having no one to split the bills or rent with). Finding love and enjoying domestic harmony is open to anyone to do in their own way, regardless of gender or orientation. So feel free to try whichever of these practices seems accessible and safe.

A final word on ethics and sustainability before we get into the good stuff. Firstly, many of the practices relate to plants and some of the suggested ingredients, once common wildflowers, are now declining or rare. Only gather from the wild if the plant is abundant, otherwise source your materials in supermarkets and garden centres or, best of all, grow them yourself to ensure a sustainable year-round supply for your charms and spells!

Second, many of the traditions in this book refer to finding out who a partner might be or seeing visions of an unspecified future beloved. You enter an ethical minefield when it comes to demanding a specific partner; there was a distaste for this kind of love magic even in earlier centuries. After all, the person you are lusting after might not be interested, or they might be into someone else. As much as it might seem like magic can solve your problems and bring you the person you want, do you really want a partner who didn't choose you freely? Besides, I'm sure you yourself wouldn't want to end up with someone you didn't choose because they magically compelled you to come to them. So if you do try the divinatory practices, do them with an open mind. If you try any of the charms and rituals, again,

keep it open and don't focus on a specific person. Let life surprise you! And yes, you could argue that the smallest action, such as bringing houseplants associated with domestic harmony into your house to improve the atmosphere, is affecting the free will of your partner. But this is where your own personal ethical code and common sense comes into play. If you're improving the atmosphere and you both benefit from it, then perhaps you can live with a nuanced approach. Above all, remember Bill and Ted's famous maxim: be excellent to each other.

Right, on to the material you came here for! There are eight chapters in this book. The first seven deal with magic and divination associated with identifying potential partners and attracting love. Given the social importance placed through history on finding love, this section is naturally bigger! The final chapter deals with rituals, traditions and practices aimed at keeping love once you've found it. Naturally, if you use any of these spells or charms and they work out for you, then I'd like an invite to the wedding!

Let's get into it!

CHAPTER 1

SEASONAL DIVINATION

Picture the scene. It is 1998 and a girl in her mid-teens sits in front of her bedroom mirror with only a candle for illumination. She holds a hairbrush in one hand, and a copy of a magazine squarely aimed at teenage girls clenched in the other. She has to tilt the page so the weak candlelight can illuminate the article that explains how to see your future boyfriend on Hallowe'en. The girl is inwardly kicking herself for not committing the practice to memory in daylight. Still, no matter, she's here now and she's going to make the most of it. She brushes her hair while staring at her reflection, hoping to see any one of a handful of boys who would be an acceptable boyfriend. She's supposed to brush her hair 100 times, and once she nears 70 strokes, she begins to wonder if she's going to see anyone, let alone the boys she had in mind. By the time she reaches 100, she has still seen no one in the mirror except herself. Deflated, and now left with hair full of static and a heart full of disappointment, she puts out the candle and goes back downstairs. She doesn't yet realize that she has participated in a lengthy tradition of Hallowe'en love divination, or that she will be writing a book about such things in 25 years' time.

This scene may or may not be familiar to you, but I'm sure it played out in countless bedrooms across the country when those magazines came out in mid-October. The articles drew on the old belief that Hallowe'en is the best time of year to practice love-life divination. The practices they described, often revolving around a desire to conjure a vision of a future partner, could be done using basic tools found around the house or items that were easy enough to source without raising an eyebrow.

Whether or not anyone else in these households knew there was a desperate teen engaging in love magic, and whether any of the rituals actually worked, is difficult to tell. What we do know is that these divinatory practices are part of a tradition dating back centuries, and yet we're still talking about them in the mid-2020s. Something about these rituals still speaks to us.

What sets the rituals in this chapter apart from the other practices we'll explore later in this book is the intention to practice them at specific times of year, such as Midsummer's Eve, Christmas Eve or New Year's Eve. Regional variations in the timing exist, so a practice conducted at Hallowe'en in one location might be central to Midsummer somewhere else.

These dates are often liminal moments in the year, straddling a change of season or marking a solar turning point, times when fairies were closer and the boundary between this world and the next became blurred. This helps to explain their interchangeable nature; you could swap one liminal date for another as the character of the time was similar.

Other magical practices are associated with saints' days, although it's not always immediately obvious why. Not all the saints involved have a connection with love and romance, but the dates must have been significant enough for the folk practices to have found their way into the written record. Other seasonal events became important in love magic too, such as new and full moons, or regular events in the social calendar such as weddings.

This chapter gives a grounding in the seasonal events most used for love magic and divination. Alternatives are noted because one practice might be done at Hallowe'en in one area and at New Year elsewhere, so you can pick and choose according to the date.

NEW MOON

The regularity of the moon's cycle makes its changing phases an excellent ritual calendar. There was a belief in Devon that you could find out the colour of your future partner's hair on the first new moon of the year. You would go outside, look for the new moon, then take off one shoe and stocking, and run across a field. On the other side of the field, you would inspect your toes. Hopefully there would be a hair between two toes to reveal the colour of your true love's hair.[8] That presupposes that you found a hair; if you didn't, you could presumably try it again the following year (or assume your partner would be bald). It's also not clear how you would interpret the results if you found hairs of more than one colour (perhaps assume multiple partners!).

Not all new moon divinations were so involved. In Berkshire, you could simply look at the new moon before bed and say,

"New moon, new moon, I hail thee!
By all the virtue in thy body,
Grant this night that I may see
He who my true love shall be!"[9]

With any luck, you would dream of your love-to-be. To achieve the same result in Ireland, people could point at the new moon with a knife and say,

**"New moon, true morrow, be true now to me,
That I to-morrow my true love may see!"[10]**

The advantage of these two practices is that they could be done on any new moon, so you had an opportunity every month to try them out!

A link between the new moon and love magic can be seen as far back as Roman times, when the new moon marked the first day of a new month. The day was referred to as the kalends and these were sacred to Juno, queen of the gods and the goddess of marriage and childbirth. While it's unlikely that folklore derives so directly from the Romans, especially in places outside their empire such as Ireland, the association between the new moon and prospective marriage partners is certainly an interesting one.

FULL MOON

While the new moon was sacred to Juno, the full moon, which marked the ides (middle) of the month, was sacred to her husband, the sky god Jupiter. When it came to love divination, it was specific full moons, at certain times of year, that were most relevant.

One such full moon was the Harvest Moon, or the full moon nearest the autumn equinox. A range of items had to be gathered beforehand. Then, at bedtime, you'd open a prayer book to the wedding service and put a key, a ring, a sprig of willow (*Salix*), a flower, a crust of bread, a heart-cake (which was shaped like a heart and contained currants and fruit peel) and some playing cards – 10 of Clubs, 9 of Hearts, Ace of Spaces and Ace of Diamonds – onto the page. Next, you'd wrap a handkerchief around the whole bundle and put it under your pillow. You'd climb into bed, cover your hands, and repeat this charm:

**"Luna, every woman's friend,
To me thy goodness condescend:
Let me this night in visions see
Emblems of my destiny."**[11]

With any luck, such a lumpy parcel under the pillow wouldn't stop you falling asleep, and you'd dream of your future partner. That this charm petitions Luna, rather than Jupiter, is telling.

Luna was the Roman goddess of the full moon, who famously fell in love with Endymion, a rather gorgeous mortal shepherd. She watched him sleep on a hillside every night, before asking Jupiter to grant him immortality so he would be beautiful forever. Luna put him into an eternal sleep so he would always stay young, although the pair somehow managed to have 50 children together (we won't ask how).

These children became the Menae, the 50 goddesses who ruled over all the lunar months within a four-year period, known as an olympiad. I'm guessing this rite was done at the time of the Harvest Moon so the practitioner can "harvest" a dream of their future. The wording of the charm suggests that even if you don't see your intended, you may yet perceive other elements of your destiny that might be just as important, if not more so!

HALLOWE'EN
(31 October)

Hallowe'en is one of the dates most associated with love divination. Many commentators cite the thinning of the veil between the worlds at this time, although this concept of the veil is largely a Victorian one. Cultures with a more animist perspective recognize the presence of spirits all year round. However, in the northern hemisphere, Hallowe'en does mark the point in the Celtic calendar when autumn gives way to winter, and this "in-between" nature marks it as a liminal time. Such moments in the year are traditionally associated with magic and intervention by spirits.

Many of the practices relate to conjuring a vision of a future husband (without allowing for the possibility that you might have more than one future husband). In one Hallowe'en ritual, women hung their smock in front of the fire as if to dry it, believing their husband-to-be would enter the room at midnight and turn the smock to dry the other side.

In an account from 1685, Scottish women dipped their smocks in water flowing south before hanging them up to dry. In some versions of the practice, the women were to hang the smock and sit up in silence until their intended's apparition arrived in a kind of waking dream.

In others, the women went straight to bed after hanging up the smock, to dream of their spouse-to-be. Elsewhere, women practiced the smock-hanging ritual on St Mark's Eve (24 April) or Midsummer's Eve (23 June). Midsummer is a time often associated with fairies, but it is unclear if they would influence the result of this particular divination, as it took place within the home, rather than in the fields or woodland where they were more usually encountered.

In *Satan's Invisible World Discovered* (1685), the Scottish Presbyterian philosophy professor George Sinclair claimed to have heard of a woman who followed this practice and, surprisingly, was visited by the likeness of a man, who turned the smock. She watched this happen from her bed, and apparently the figure crossed the room and kissed her. In Sinclair's view, this was clearly the Devil, something the woman herself didn't recognize, although given Sinclair's book was an attempt to prove Satan's existence through collecting "true" stories, we can see where he's coming from here.[12] Sadly, he did not record if the woman went on to marry the man she saw in her vision.

By the mid-19th century, some young women were hanging their inside-out chemises on a hedge. Whoever came along and turned their undergarments the right way out would be their future husband, which suggests they would need to keep watch to see who appeared.[13] This version of the practice was clearly open to external manipulation, if any ne'er-do-well young men wanted to con a young woman into marrying them.

Also popular at Hallowe'en was the baking of the "dumb cake", which had to be made in absolute silence. In modern ears, "dumb" sounds like an ableist term, so let's use its other name – "silent cake". The practice was first recorded in the 1680s, although various recipes and methods have appeared over the years and in different regions – earlier ingredients included soot and urine, which thankfully disappeared from later versions.

Certain elements remain the same, such as having several people make the cake together, and always in total silence. A silent cake also nearly always included a lot of salt, and was broken into portions that participants marked with their initials, and then was either put under a pillow or eaten before bed.[14] The goal was to conjure either a vision or a dream of a future husband.

Sinclair proclaimed that young women in the Scottish Highlands went to bed in silence on Hallowe'en, having made and eaten a cake out of soot, in order to dream of their husband-to-be. He wouldn't be drawn on whether such a practice involved actual magic, but he wasn't keen on it either way.[15] It does suggest that the young women were desperate to know their romantic futures if they were willing to eat soot, though there's also the possibility that those who recorded the original recipes altered the ingredients to put people off making them.

Girls most often made silent cakes at Hallowe'en or on Christmas Eve, St Agnes' Eve or Midsummer's Eve – notable points in the calendar for marriage divination. The tradition seems to have largely died out by the end of the 19th century, perhaps due to its complexity (or maybe people just didn't want to eat soot).

The description of silent cake-baking in northern England recorded by 19th-century folklorist William Henderson gives you an example of how convoluted the process could be. Two young women chose to make their silent cake on St Agnes' Eve (which we'll examine in more detail later in the chapter). They spent the entire day in silence, eating and drinking nothing, before making the cake in the evening. In the spirit of the divination, the girls divided the tasks equally between them. They used equal proportions of flour, salt and water to create a flat salt dough. After removing it from the oven, they cut the cake in half, and each girl walked backward upstairs with her half. Finally, both girls ate their portion and jumped into bed. If they'd done it right, and kept their thoughts focused on a husband, each girl would see her future love in her dreams.[16] Henderson doesn't elaborate on whether anyone was ever actually successful, but I can't imagine eating a cake made with that much salt would be particularly pleasant.

Henderson also noted a variation in which the girls made the cakes in thimbles, so they were easier to eat. After all, if you're eating baked salt dough, you don't want to force yourself through a huge wedge of it. When the girls got into  bed, they laid out their stockings in a cross and put their shoes in the "coming and going" position; in other words, with one shoe facing away and the other pointing toward them. This variation covers a range of practices designed to promote prophetic dreams, so if the girls did dream of a future husband, it would be difficult to know which part of the divination had worked, but using so many practices at once made it more likely that it might work.

One Hallowe'en practice that is far less well-known today, and which men as well as women took part in, involved using three dishes to divine your romantic future. It was easy to do at social gatherings and sounds like a good party game. The host sent those intending to take part out of the room and placed three dishes on a table. One contained clean water, one held dirty water and the third was empty. The participants put on blindfolds and the host led them back into the room, having mixed up the dishes. The blindfolded players then dipped their left hand into one of the dishes. Dipping your hand in clean water meant you would marry a virgin, while choosing the muddy water meant you would marry a widow or a widower. Anyone who chose the empty basin would never marry at all. The process was repeated twice more, with the dishes mixed up each time.[17] Robert Burns mentions this practice in a note to his 1785 poem "Halloween". It's unclear what the result would be if you chose a different dish each time!

A version from 1890s Gloucestershire appears to have been aimed at children. The adults set up three plates containing either a gold item, a ring or a thimble. The children were blindfolded and directed toward the plates. If they grasped the gold item, they would have a rich marriage. The ring signified an early marriage, and the thimble meant no marriage at all.[18] It's possible that the thimble was associated with singlehood because it suggested an occupation – either as a seamstress or a tailor – rather than marriage as a source of income. It also suggests this tradition was a middle-class one, as working-class people didn't stop working when they married. I won't comment on the use of this game to make children aware of the importance of a good marriage, but it could be fun to adapt this one to add something a little different to your Hallowe'en house parties.

ST BARBARA'S DAY
(4 December)

On 4 December, St Barbara's Day, it was a custom in Austria and southern Germany for village girls to gather fruit-tree branches. Each girl took one of the branches to keep safe. On Christmas Day, they brought out the branches to see if any had put out buds. If they had, this meant the harvest would be good. Whichever girl's branch had put out buds first would be the first to marry. In some places, young men kept the branches in a heated room to force them into flower, giving them as presents to their sweethearts.[19]

St Barbara is a strange choice to petition for romantic matters. Her father locked her in a tower in Heliopolis sometime in the 3rd century CE to prevent men from seeing her beauty. He was furious to discover she was a Christian and handed her to the authorities. They tortured her to force her to recant her faith but when her wounds miraculously healed every night, they finally sentenced her to death. After her execution, her torturers were struck by lightning.[20] Since then, St Barbara has been the patron saint of armourers, military engineers, miners and anyone who works with explosives. I can't quite see the connection to romantic divination!

ST THOMAS'S EVE (20 December)

If you'd missed the opportunities for prophetic dreams on Hallowe'en, you could wait until St Thomas's Eve on 20 December to try again. This practice involved using an onion to see a vision of your true love, though I'm unsure why onions would be applicable in a love divination, as opposed to something like an apple, which has a long association with love and relationships. (The link between onions and crying is what immediately springs to mind, but I hesitate to suggest this!) If you wanted to perform this rite, you had to buy your onion in a very specific way, going into the greengrocer's by one door and leaving by another. It's not explained where the different doors are (presumably in the actual shop) or what to do if the greengrocer's only had one door. If you followed this method correctly and put the onion under your pillow on St Thomas's Eve, you would see your true love in your dreams.[21]

It's unclear why you would do this on St Thomas's Eve. The phrase "doubting Thomas" came from his request for proof of Christ's resurrection, and he's the patron saint of architects and judges. Like St Barbara, he doesn't have much of an obvious connection to love or romance. Or onions, for that matter.

CHRISTMAS EVE (24 December)

Another opportunity for prophetic dreams came later that week. Girls could pick 12 leaves of common sage (*Salvia officinalis*) at midnight on Christmas Eve to see a vision of their future husband. In Lincolnshire, the same practice involved red sage (*Salvia miltiorrhiza*) and was done on St Mark's Eve (24 April) rather than at Christmas. Either way, it was specified that you had to be careful not to damage the bush during your foraging.[22] If you opted for doing this on Christmas Eve, you could always use the sage leaves in your Christmas dinner. (If trying this out in North America, avoid using the endangered white sage, *Salvia apiana*.)

✦ NEW YEAR'S EVE (31 December) ✦

On the night of New Year's Eve, an unmarried girl had nine attempts to throw her shoe at a willow. If it stayed among the branches, she'd marry that year.[23] If the shoe fell out the tree, then she would not marry that year. If you were unsuccessful on New Year's Eve, you could always have another go at Easter.

I can't help thinking this could form the plot of an excellent rom-com, with a hapless romantic accidentally knocking out her future suitor with a sandal thrown at a willow in the garden. She helps him over his concussion and love eventually blossoms ... along with a nasty bruise.

There was also a practice designed for New Year's Day, recorded in a 16th-century household notebook in Northamptonshire. Anyone wanting to know who they would marry was directed to "sow" hemp seed (*Cannabis sativa*) around their fire on New Year's Day, while reciting a rhyme:

**"Hemp seed, hemp I sow thee,
lead and un-lead.
She that shall be my world,
come after me and rake,
Sleep, sleep, and I see her, wake and know her."**[24]

No, it's not the catchiest verse, but it was originally written in 16th-century English, so the language is somewhat archaic. Following the rhyme, they should go to bed, lying on their right side, and speak only to recite their prayers. If all went well, they would dream of their future wife or husband.

ST AGNES' EVE
(20 January)

The Eve of St Agnes (20 January) was a traditional time to practice various rituals before bed to dream of your future partner. St Agnes lived in Rome in the 4th century. Wanting to devote herself to her religion, she refused a marriage proposal from the son of a Roman prefect, who in a fit of spite reported her as a Christian. The authorities arrested Agnes and sentenced her to work in a public brothel. According to legend, God intervened and every man who tried to rape her immediately went blind. As the punishment had failed to make her give up Christianity, she was accused of witchcraft, but when she was tied to the stake, the wood would not burn. Eventually, they resorted to beheading her and she died in 304 CE at the age of 12 or 13. Agnes became the patron saint of virgins, chastity and girls, and is also the saint for victims of rape.

John Keats wrote "The Eve of St Agnes" in 1820, a poem that tells the story of Porphyro, a young man who hopes to sneak into the bedroom of his beloved, Madeline, on St Agnes' Eve. Madeline's old nurse smuggles Porphyro into the room, and when Madeline wakes in the night, she believes him to be a vision of her future husband and welcomes him into her bed. She realizes her error in the morning when her vision is still there, but they run away together and presumably enjoy a happy-ever-after.

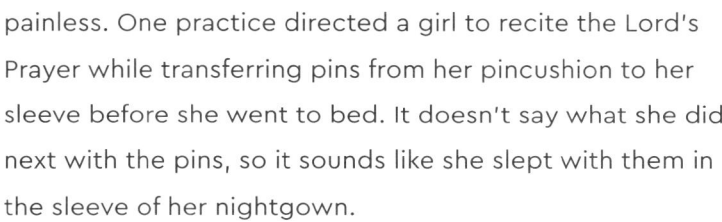

The rituals to induce dreams of future partners on St Agnes' Eve weren't always painless. One practice directed a girl to recite the Lord's Prayer while transferring pins from her pincushion to her sleeve before she went to bed. It doesn't say what she did next with the pins, so it sounds like she slept with them in the sleeve of her nightgown.

According to another ritual, she needed to walk backward up the stairs when she retired to bed that evening. Fasting for the whole day was a further option, as was making a silent cake with friends, described earlier in the Hallowe'en section (see page 31).[25]

An easier approach involved a pair of shoes, plus some thyme (Thymus vulgaris) and rosemary (Rosmarinus officinalis). Both plants are easy to grow or source from supermarkets if you want to try this one for yourself, and you don't need the flowers, so seasonality is not an issue. A girl would put a thyme leaf in one shoe, and a rosemary sprig in the other, then place a shoe on either side of the bed while reciting this charm:

> **"St Agnes, that's to lovers kind,**
> **Come, ease the trouble of my mind."**

With any luck, she would dream of the person she would inevitably marry.[26]

In Scotland, girls gathered in crop fields on St Agnes' Eve and would throw a handful of grain onto the bare soil at the stroke of midnight. They would recite this charm:

> **"Agnes sweet and Agnes fair,**
> **hither, hither, now repair;**
> **Bonny Agnes, let me see**
> **the lad who is to marry me".[27]**

The charm doesn't specify whether they expected to see their intended in a dream or in a vision there and then, but it's likely they meant in a dream, having "repaired" to bed.

ST VALENTINE'S DAY
(14 February)

Trying to divine the origins of Valentine's Day proves challenging. Some believe the day is named for St Valentine, a Roman priest who conducted marriage ceremonies in secret in defiance of the emperor's ban and who was executed once his clandestine weddings were discovered. Others think it derives from the Roman fertility festival of Lupercalia, held on 13–15 February, which was renamed in 496 CE by Pope Gelasius, claiming St Valentine died refusing to recant his Christianity. If true, the change removed the pagan roots of the festival and turned it into a Christian celebration of love. Perhaps its origins no longer matter, given how firmly associated the day has become with love and romance!

In terms of folklore, one belief claimed women would fall head over heels for the first person they saw on Valentine's Day. Some women apparently manufactured early morning encounters with men who'd caught their eye. Samuel Pepys even recorded in his diary in 1662 that his wife kept her hand over her eyes while she moved around their house to avoid seeing the workmen doing renovations. You can imagine that this belief might be rife with skulduggery!

We've looked at various practices involving seeking a vision of your intended, and Valentine's Day was no exception. The night before Valentine's Day, you should head to a cemetery and at precisely midnight run around the church 12 times. If you did it properly, the likeness of your future lover would appear. Others believed you'd see omens (rather than a vision) that you'd have to interpret to reveal your partner-to-be.

We'll cover the other major practice for Valentine's Day, called ornithomancy, in Chapter 5 on love omens, because it involves a spot of birdwatching – perfect for our animal-related practices!

EASTER

Love divination was not reserved for the unpartnered seeking information about their romantic future, as you might do at Easter by throwing your shoe at a willow tree. Those in relationships could also use divination at Easter to check if their lover was faithful. For this ritual, the suspicious lover ate an apple on Easter Sunday as soon as they woke up. While eating, they had to say,

"As Eve in her thirst for knowledge ate
So I too, thirst to know my fate."

Then they'd count the apple seeds. An even number meant their lover was true, while an odd number meant their love was false.[28]

ST MARK'S EVE
(24 April)

Even grass could be used to foresee whether you would be single or married, and this next practice also gives information on your fortunes in general. You were directed to go to the churchyard at midnight on St Mark's Eve (24 April) and find a grave on the south side. There, you would pull three tufts of grass, go home and put the grass under your pillow. Before going to sleep you would recite this charm three times:

> **"The Eve of St Mark by prediction is blest,**
> **Set therefore my hopes and my fears all to rest;**
> **Let me know my fate, whether weal or woe,**
> **Whether my rank is to be high or low;**
> **Whether to live single or to be a bride,**
> **And the destiny my star doth provide."**

If the charm worked, your dream would reveal if you'd find a partner, and whether you would be rich or poor as a result. If you dreamed of nothing, you'd remain single and be miserable.[29] I can only assume singlehood was equated with misery due to the financial precarity of not having a marriage partner.

MIDSUMMER'S EVE (23 June)

Midsummer's Eve is sometimes confused with the summer solstice, as they fall within days of one another. The summer solstice marks the longest day of the year and is an astronomical event that can fall on 20, 21 or 22 June. Midsummer's Day always falls on 24 June and is also known as St John's Day. Midsummer also marked one of the quarter days in England when rents were due, and servants might be hired or fired. It was a day associated with the fairies in many parts of Europe. In Romania, for example, people left offerings for the benevolent fairies that would pass by that night.[30] Naturally, such a seemingly magical day accrued a range of divinatory possibilities.

In the Midlands and northern England, a girl would put a sprig of myrtle (*Myrtus communis*) on her open prayer book on St John's Eve (23 June). She'd ask, "Wilt thou take me to be thy wedded wife?" while doing so. Then she'd close the book and put it under her pillow. If the myrtle was gone in the morning, she'd marry her sweetheart.[31] Given the association between myrtle and weddings in the Victorian period (see page 226), the choice of flower makes sense.

Those girls hoping for a little more information about a prospective partner might put a dish of flour under a rosemary bush on Midsummer's Eve. They'd eagerly check it in the morning to see if their future husband's initials had been written in the flour.[32] I can imagine their disappointment if they checked the dish and found the flour untouched or marked with something indecipherable. If I tried that where I live, I'd no doubt find nothing but hedgehog paw prints!

To induce prophetic dreams of a partner on Midsummer's Eve, girls in England would also take their shoes and form them in the shape of a T – so one shoe made the vertical stem, and the other shoe made the horizontal bar. Then they would repeat this rhyme:

"I place my shoes like a letter T,
In hopes my true love I shall see,
In his apparel and his array,
As he is now and every day."[33]

Then they had to swap the shoes over, so one was now the bar and the other the stem, and repeat the charm, before reversing them again and saying it a third time. I tried this practice for the purposes of this book and I'm sad to say that I couldn't remember what I'd dreamed about. In all fairness, though, that doesn't mean I didn't dream of my true love – just that I don't remember doing so!

Sometimes an unmarried woman would fast all day on Midsummer's Eve and then lay out a spread of bread, cheese and ale on a table covered in a clean cloth. She would leave open the street door and sit at the table, where she would prepare to eat. At midnight, a vision of the man she would marry would come in, bow to her, pour a glass of ale, bow again and leave.[34] With the street door standing open, it

is possible that men who knew of the custom might sneak into women's houses to masquerade as a waking vision of their true love. Presumably women knew how to tell the difference.

The more energetic single woman could head to a churchyard on Midsummer Eve to conjure a waking vision of her love-to-be. At the stroke of midnight, she would run around the church scattering rose leaves and rosemary, chanting,

**"Rose leaves, rose leaves, rose leaves I strew,
He that will love me, come after me now."[35]**

She would then wait to see a vision of her intended – though how many girls simply ended up getting a fright in a dark churchyard is unknown. This practice is an adapted version of the "sowing hemp seed around the fire" rite from New Year's Day. Some time between the 16th and 19th centuries, it moved from being practiced on New Year's Day to Midsummer's Eve, and the elements of silence, prayers and fire disappeared from the rite. While the roses used at Midsummer's Eve make sense in a love charm, the New Year's Day inclusion of hemp might reference the use of this plant to make rope, thus "binding" the couple.[36]

This practice was even mirrored by a version for young men. On Midsummer's Eve, they should circle a church at midnight three or nine times with a drawn sword, saying, "Here's the sword, but where's the scabbard?"[37] This somewhat crude spoken charm was intended to conjure a vision of their intended sweetheart.

In Sweden, girls gathered flowers from nine different locations on St John's Eve for their love divination. One of these plants had to be St John's wort *(Hypericum perforatum)*, which blooms at this time of year. She would then make a bouquet of the collected flowers and put it under her pillow to dream

of her intended partner, who with any luck would soon enter her life. Given the other eight plants are not named, this is a wonderfully flexible dream divination to try using sustainable common flowers.

If a girl wanted to call in a partner, rather than see who the partner would be, a ritual from Yorkshire directed her to gather 12 sage leaves *(Salvia officinalis)* at midnight on Midsummer's Eve. She was to put them in a saucer and then leave that in a drawer all day until the following midnight. Just before 12, she should open the window and drop a leaf outside for every stroke of the hour. This would summon a husband to her home.[38]

In Ireland, people lit bonfires on Midsummer's Eve in honour of Áine, the fairy queen and goddess of love and summer (among other things). A couple would jump over the fire while holding hands, and if they let go of each other, it meant the relationship would end.[39]

ST LUKE'S DAY
(18 October)

On St Luke's Day (18 October), girls ground marigold flowers (*Tagetes*), thyme (*Thymus vulgaris*), wormwood (*Artemisia absinthium*) and marjoram (*Origanum majorana*) to powder. They'd add this to honey and vinegar and warm it over the fire. Finally, they'd anoint themselves with the mixture at bedtime, saying,

**"St Luke, St Luke, be kind to me,
In dreams let me my true love see."**[40]

It's possible the wormwood was intended to provide noteworthy dreams through its traditional links with hallucinations.

Herbal teas and infusions also offered prophetic possibilities. Tudor girls would drink lavender (*Lavandula*) tea before bed, asking St Luke to bring a vision of their true love in their dreams. St Luke is an interesting choice as a figure to petition, as he was the patron saint of physicians and surgeons; much like St Barbara and St Thomas, he's not an obvious figure to ask for help in the romance department.

WEDDING DIVINATIONS

Finally, rather than being dictated by calendar date, one subset of divinatory practices is linked to a very specific event. Yes, we're talking wedding rituals!

Just think of the practice of throwing the bouquet to determine who will get married next. This ritual has become a pop culture trope, with female characters in movies fighting to be the one to catch the bouquet, and it's even spawned a meme that suggests you have someone throw the wreath at your funeral to determine who is the next to die. This ritual turns the wedding bouquet into a sort of baton that the bride passes on to the next single woman in the giant marriage relay of life.

My personal favourite marriage divination involves the wedding cake, because, well, it's cake. Wedding cake was recorded as an ingredient in love divinations from the early 18th century.[41] The bride would pass small fragments of cake through her wedding ring nine times. She then handed these out to unmarried women who would place the piece under their pillow to dream of their future partner.[42] It's likely the passage of the cake through the ring was intended to charge it with the bride's "success" in marriage. And if a bride didn't finish her slice of cake and a single person finished it for her, it was a sign they too would marry soon.[43]

One incredibly specific multi-part omen involved cheese. The bride cut a piece of cheese before she left the wedding table and the woman she gave it to would be the next bride. After the dinner, the designated bride-to-be stuck her knife into the cheese. Everyone scrabbled to grab it, and whoever did so without cutting their fingers would have happiness in their married life. If the best man failed to grab it, he'd be unlucky in marriage.[44]

'WHICH WILL YOU TRY?

There is a clear focus in the seasonal practices described above on conjuring a vision of your love-to-be, either while awake or asleep. While it's not clear how many people did actually see a partner in a vision or a dream – much less go on to marry them – we do have George Sinclair's assertion that at least one woman saw such a vision.

At least the distribution of the practices throughout the year gives several opportunities to try them out, which could lessen the sting if you get no discernible results on the first or second try. Perhaps these practices are perhaps more about providing comfort, reassuring you that there is a partner in your future, rather than providing certainty about who it is.

What's harder to understand is why many of these saints became linked with the practices, given that there is no obvious association between them and love or romance. It's always possible it was the date itself that was more important. Perhaps local customs on these saints' feast days lent themselves to the traditions.

CHAPTER 2

WISHES, SPELLS & CHARMS

While many of the methods we'll discuss in this book involve divination to discover who (if anyone) you might end up with, in this chapter, we'll focus on magic. After all, divination might give you information about your partner-to-be, but magic lets you take action in bringing them to your door. There's no guarantee that magic will work as there are so many variables, such as free will, the availability of potential partners and your talent for magic making. But choosing when and how to cast a spell could give you some say in the love-finding process!

While dating might feel like a thankless task in an era of constant swiping, ghosting, catfishing and other unpleasant contemporary behaviours, imagine how hard it would have been as a 17th-century servant! Your dating pool would have been limited to the singletons of your class in your local area. It's easy to see why people might turn to magic.

Some of these practices would have been beyond the means of an ordinary person in earlier centuries, but I've included them so you can see how deep the desire for love ran. We'll explore a range of magic, including making wishes, casting spells and using love potions and charms. Remember my previous note about ethics: keep it general and don't target specific people. After all, someone who looks like a good idea on paper might be a terrible match for you in person!

WISHES

We're well-versed in making wishes from a young age. After all, we're told to make a wish every time we blow out our birthday cake candles. And how many children will have looked out their window, sought out the first pinprick of silvery light in the sky and repeated the following rhyme?

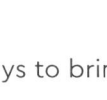

> **"Star light, star bright,**
> **First star I see tonight,**
> **I wish I may, I wish I might,**
> **Have this wish I wish tonight."**

It's hardly surprising that one of the simplest ways to bring love into your life is wishing for it. But this is folklore we're talking about, so there's going to be a little more to the process than simply making a wish (though nothing is stopping you from doing that too).

Wishing wells are a well-known concept, even if our use of them has dwindled to throwing pennies into shopping centre fountains. The first record of "wishing well" in the *Oxford English Dictionary* comes from 1792, but it's likely that the term relates to the centuries-old practice of people making offerings at holy or healing wells. There is a Gloucestershire legend, for example, of Romans throwing silver coins into water whenever they crossed a river, lake, sea or stream.[45] In earlier times, people would have made a journey to an appropriate well to make a wish, often on a specified day, such as Midsummer's Eve. It wouldn't be just any well; most wells were dedicated to saints, and some were even associated with cursing. If you wanted to make a wish, you would need a well associated with wishing, meaning you would need to *really* want to make the wish to go to the effort of reaching the well.

Head to the county of Northumberland in northern England, to the small town of Wooler at the foot of the beautiful Cheviot Hills. A footpath from the town heads up the hill toward the Pin Well, or Fairy's Well, which is famous for its wish-granting abilities. Banish any mental image of the type of well you get in fairy tales, with a round shaft and a wooden cap containing the winding mechanism, because the Pin Well is just a rough basin of large granite stones. In the 19th century, it would also have boasted a collection of crooked pins ranging from the very rusty to the brand new.[46]

As the belief went, you visited the well on May Day when you bent a pin and dropped it into the well while making your wish. The pin acted as an offering to the fairies, who with luck would then grant said wish. It was young women hoping for a husband who most often made use of the practice. I have heard it said that the fairies used the pins as arrows, which explains why they looked on pins so favourably as offerings. Regarding their crookedness, there's a theory they had to be "broken" to be an offering, and bending pins is the easiest way to do that.

Across the north of England, passersby might breathe their wish as they passed a wishing well. It was important to drop a crooked pin into the well as "payment" to ensure the wish came true.[47]

This practice is associated with a range of wells associated with healing, which were also popular for those seeking love. At the well of St John at Mount Grace Priory in North Yorkshire, hopeful people stuck a pin through an ivy leaf (*Hedera helix*) before floating it on the water to make their wish. Leaves that floated meant the wish would come true; leaves that sank meant the wish would go ungranted.[48] I can only imagine how someone felt when their leaf wishing for a partner sank.

People at St Anne's Well in Trellech in Monmouthshire offered a pebble with their wish. If lots of bubbles appeared when they dropped the pebble into the water, their wish would be granted. A few bubbles meant a granted wish after a delay. If no bubbles appeared, their wish was denied.[49]

Sometimes the process was much more convoluted than simply dropping a pin into the water. One tradition about St Mary's Well near Aberdaron on the Llyn Peninsula, Wales, said that a beautiful woman wanted to make a wish. A strange woman visited her one day at sunset, telling her she would get her wish if she went down to the well, filled her mouth with water, came back up and then walked a circuit around the church without spilling a drop. The story doesn't say if she managed it, but according to legend young people continued to try the ritual to get their wishes granted.[50] If you were desperate to find love, you might just give it a go. After all, it didn't cost anything except your time.

A variation on the wishing well practice was recorded in 1955 in Italy, on the Amalfi Coast. Lovelorn women would visit the Il Pirata grotto at night, and under the moonlight throw three pebbles at a rock sticking out of the water. It didn't actually matter if they hit the rock or not, it was simply important that they throw the three stones to meet the man of their dreams.

Some locals reported it could help if they named a man or two that they had their eye on while tossing the pebbles, and claimed that people seldom had to visit the grotto a second time. The account noted that there were "few old maids" in the area, suggesting that the superstition worked after all.[51] Perhaps I should crowdfund a trip there. You know, for research ...

Of course, you don't need a well to make a wish. In Oxfordshire, the Uffington White Horse chalk hill figure is believed to have been associated with wish-making superstitions. All you needed to do was stand on the horse's eye while making your wish and it would come true.[52] There's no way to know how old a superstition like this is, especially as the chalk horse has been scientifically dated back to the Bronze Age, but it just goes to show that people will find ways to magically interact with ancient or unusual monuments. This superstition isn't specifically related to love magic, but I imagine many people would have made wishes to find love, bring back straying partners or even bring down misfortune onto an ex!

If you don't live near a well or the Uffington White Horse, the humble dandelion (*Taraxacum officinale*) is a common plant that offers a simple way to make wishes. It's difficult to tell where dandelion lore originated since these practices have been so often repeated. Blow on the seedhead to dislodge the seed and make a wish as you do so. Perhaps people thought this worked because blowing the seeds sent your wish out into the world, or because – given how prolific dandelions are and how deep their roots go – the wish would "take root" when the seeds did.

Some versions of the lore state that your wish will only come true if you blow all the seeds off the seedhead. You could also picture a message to a loved one and then blow on a seedhead in their direction to send them the message.[53] In Aberdeen, it was the seeds that were important, not the act of blowing on the seedhead. The seeds were called "hairy witches" and you could make a wish on it if you caught one.[54] So you didn't have to be the one to blow on the seedhead to get the benefit of it.

If you want to make a wish to find love and check if it'll come true, and you don't have a handy wishing well nearby, you can use playing cards instead. We'll talk more about using playing cards for divination in Chapter 7, but for now all you need is a deck of cards.

Cut the deck and make a note of the card you see. Make your wish; let's say it's to meet a compatible partner. Now, shuffle the cards and cut the deck into three piles. Sort through each pile looking for the card you saw. If it's in the first pile, your wish will come true. You'll get it after a longer period if it's in the second pile, but it won't come true if it's in the third pile.[55] Naturally, I decided to try this out for the purposes of this book. When I cut the deck, my card was the 2 of Diamonds, and I found it in the second pile. Win!

SPELLS

Wishes are probably the most basic form of spellcasting, but spells can be far more complicated, involving specific actions, unusual ingredients or incantations. Love is frequently mentioned in Roman magic, and a very early example of a love spell in Greek literature comes from the second Idyll of Theocritus, a poet working in the 3rd century. In the poem, Simaetha wants to bring back her errant lover Delphis, who has been gone for 12 days. We can only guess at Delphis's intentions because Simaetha laments that he didn't make her his wife but has not left her a maiden – this could be an ancient record of being ghosted by a one-night stand. She calls upon the goddess Hecate for help on a full moon.

The moon phase is important as it refers to the *Dea Triformis*, or the three moon goddesses. The first is Selene in the heavens, the second is Artemis on earth and the third is Hecate in the underworld. Performing this charm was intended to compel the moon goddess to appear and do whatever the magician wanted.[56] It is notable that she's calling upon Hecate, given her role as the goddess of witchcraft, magic and the underworld.

During the rite, Simaetha's servant Thestylis burns barley (*Hordeum vulgare*) meal, bay (*Laurus nobilis*) leaves, a wax image of Delphis and then bran. While Thestylis does so, Simaetha spins a brass wryneck, which is a four-spoked wheel, sometimes also referred to as an iynx. Spinning this wheel not only produces a pleasing sound, but was also believed to help draw an errant lover back, or to draw a lover to the user. As Simaetha spins the wheel, she repeats the refrain, "Wryneck, wryneck, draw him hither".

When she hears Hecate approach, she beats a brass pan for the goddess and pours her libations as an offering. She begs Hecate to bring Delphis to her door, before burning a plant referred to as "horse-madness" and the fringe from Delphis's cloak. Simaetha then sends Thestylis off with the ashes of all they have burned, with the instructions that she should smear them on the lintel above Delphis's door, spit once and say, "Delphis's bones I smear".[57]

It's unclear if Simaetha thinks her ritual will work, especially when she says she'll go to see Delphis to ask him what he's playing at, but it feels as though her monologue to the moon would have been at least therapeutic, if nothing else.

The iynx, or a spoked wheel with a wryneck bird attached to it, was associated with love magic from the time of the original Greek myths in which it appeared. In these stories, Iynx was the nymph who compelled Zeus to fall in love with her (or, in other versions of the myth, with Io, another nymph). A furious Hera then turned Iynx into a wryneck. Aphrodite gave Jason (of Jason and the Argonauts fame)

an iynx wheel which he used to arouse the passions of the enchantress Medea.[58]

Due to the iynx's links with love magic, both Aphrodite and Eros sometimes carry one in ancient depictions of them. Look for a small wheel on a string. The iynx eventually disappeared from magical literature (later reappearing as a way to invoke deities), which is a shame as they're easy to make and use.

Source a spinner in a toy store or use a really large button (a couple of inches wide, at least) or punch two holes near each other in the centre of a thin wood or metal disc. Thread a 1.5m (2ft) length of string through the holes and knot the ends together to make a loop. Hold an end of the loop in each hand and let the disc settle in the middle. Keeping one hand still, rotate the other wrist to wind the string in one direction. When you hit the right tension, you let go and gently pull on each end of the loop while the disc spins. Move your hands closer together before it fully unwinds, and it will start to wind in the other direction. Keep doing this for as long as you need to while repeating whatever prayers, chants or spells are helpful to you in your quest for love.

It's impossible to know if the ancient practitioners believed these spells would work. Occasionally we find record of something similar in more recent folklore.

In the late 18th century, Passon Harris, a former vicar in Hennock, south Devon, was reported to have cast a spell on behalf of his housemaid. Harris had discovered that his maid's lover had abandoned her the week before and gone to the north of the county, leaving her bereft.

Apparently, he had a knack for using spells to recover stolen property, so he cast one to bring back the young man. Harris believed he'd return before the following evening, although the spell didn't work initially because the young man had his prayerbook in his coat pocket, ready for church. The spell only took effect when he undressed for bed that night, when the young man found himself compelled to reach his former lover. He ran all night back to Hennock, and the maid found him panting on the doorstep the next morning.[59] Unfortunately, the folklore doesn't record the results of the spell, or whether the reconciliation was permanent, but it's fascinating to see such magic being worked by a former vicar!

ENCHANTED RINGS

While this book is largely focused on the folk magic accessible to ordinary people, love magic also appeared in more literary or "serious" occult texts, including works of astrological magic calling on the celestial spheres for their influence in particular matters. *De Imaginibus et Horis* ("on the images and hours") was a 12th-century Arabic text that was translated into Latin, like many other important works that only became available in Europe following their translation. Attributed to Hermes, this book included instructions for making magical rings for various purposes. One of them was designed to make the person you fancied fall in love with you, regardless of whether they were already married or not, or even liked you. I suppose the type of magical practitioner who wouldn't baulk at demanding things from spirits would have no problem with ignoring a human's consent.

The instructions are fairly intensive, so would only have been accessible to literate and magically operative practitioners, and of course there's no way to know how many people ever actually made this ring. At sunrise on a Friday, the day and hour ruled by the planet Venus, the magician needed to carve a hyacinth stone with an image of a woman holding a comb in her right hand and an apple in her left (combs and apples both being associated with the goddess Venus). Hyacinth, also called jacinth, is a type of zircon that comes in red, yellow or orange varieties.

Then, again working immediately after sunrise on a Friday, the magician would make a ring and set the stone in it, to turn it into a seal. The time after sunrise on Friday is a planetary hour associated with Venus, which in astrological magic means that the power of Venus is amplified – Venus's influence would be far stronger during her hour on her day than if you called upon her during a different planetary hour on a different day.

Planetary hours divide up the hours of daylight and darkness, and associate each segment with (in this order, but starting with a different planet every day) Saturn, Jupiter, Mars, the Sun, Venus, Mercury and the Moon. A new planetary day begins at sunrise and ends the following sunrise, so the timing of the planetary hours varies according to the time of sunrise in your location. The length of a planetary hour varies too; only at equinox is a planetary hour 60 minutes long, because each period of daylight or darkness is divided by 12 to obtain a planetary hour of the day or of the night. Thankfully, calculators are available online to tell you the planetary hour in your specific location.

Some people arrange their activities according to the planetary day (doing business admin on a Wednesday, the day associated with Mercury, for example, or self-care work on Friday, the day associated with Venus), and I've even seen people arrange their to-do list according to planetary hour.

On a Friday, the first of Venus's planetary hours is always the period after sunrise (though as discussed above it wouldn't usually be 60 minutes long), and there is a second Venus planetary hour during daylight, and two more at night.

Next, the magician recited angel names during Venus's planetary hour for eight days (when these hours fall varied depending on the day of the week). Once they'd done all of this, they would bathe the ring in aloe smoke and put it in a clay vessel with frankincense resin. At this point, the ring was finished.

To work the magic, the magician carved certain characters in wax and then pressed the inscribed hyacinth stone into the wax too, to impress the image of the woman with the apple and comb. Finally, they broke the wax into pieces and put one in the drink of the person they wanted to love them.[60] As you can see, the whole process was very involved, and presumably beyond the reach of most people.

Modern magical practitioners do make and sell astrological talismans, saving us from having to make our own. These talismans are made during an "election", a time chosen for its beneficial astrological impact, and suffumigated with the appropriate incense. These contemporary versions are designed to attract things to you, such as love, prosperity or luck, rather than to compel others to do anything. They're more like magical magnets for the things you'd like more of in your life.

LOVE POTIONS

The 12th-century chivalric romance of Tristan and Iseult centres around a love potion. In the tale, Cornish knight Tristan is charged with escorting Irish princess Iseult to Cornwall where she will marry his uncle, King Mark. In some variations of the legend, Iseult's mother gives her the potion to use on her wedding night, and in others, the potion maker instructs Iseult in sharing the potion with Mark. Whether on purpose or by accident, Tristan and Iseult end up taking the potion, and they fall in love with each other. Iseult goes on to marry Mark anyway, but she continues to seek out Tristan. In some versions, the love potion wears off eventually (sometimes specified as a period of three years), while in others, it lasts for a lifetime. As romantic as it might sound, nothing good really comes of them taking the potion.

In many ways, this sums up the problem with love potions. What do you do when they wear off? What do you do if they *don't* wear off? How do you persuade the other person to take it? What if the person you're madly in love with isn't quite what you hope for after they take the potion? Can you *reverse* a love potion?

Despite these questions, love potions, or philtres, were used from the Middle Ages until the 17th century when spells and

charms overtook them in popularity. Potions fell from favour mostly because they were more complicated than spells or charms to administer. On paper, they were straightforward: you chose the person you wanted to fall in love with you and gave them the philtre to drink.

Roman biographer Suetonius claimed Caligula drank a love philtre given by his wife Caesonia, except it drove him mad instead.[61] Yet in reality, it wasn't easy to get someone to take a philtre, especially if you didn't know them well enough to have reason to give them something to drink. I'm sure people may have gotten suspicious if you'd tried to ply them with drink for no apparent reason, much as we'd be suspicious of such an action today.

Yet love potions are still fascinating, with a glamorous portrayal in art and literature that goes beyond the legend of Tristan and Iseult. The 1903 painting "The Love Potion" by Evelyn De Morgan, for example, illustrates the crafting of such potions, with the sorceress depicted more as an alchemist, surrounded by books.

The embracing couple in the background could be former clients of hers, brought together by a potion similar to the one that she mixes in the foreground. And then there's the juice squeezed from the flower struck by Cupid's arrow in Shakespeare's 1600 play *A Midsummer Night's Dream*: a form of love potion that creates chaos for the characters involved.

Love potions even appear in the historical record. Despite being a famous beauty at the French court, Madame Athenais de Montespan was unable to seduce King Louis XIV. After she struck up a friendship with the queen and was invited to dinner with the couple, however, the king had a change of heart. Rumour had it that Montespan had spiked Louis' food with various love potions, some of which included blood, intestines and toad parts, with help from the sorceress Catherine Monvoisin. Montespan ended up being mother to seven of the king's children, so her potions apparently worked.[62] She also subjected herself to a dazzling array of pomades, lotions and other beauty products, which brings a whole new meaning to the concept of the love potion.

Not all potions involved disgusting ingredients. Many philtre recipes started out with a base of wine, tea or water, with the addition of herbs and other ingredients. Mandrake (*Mandragora officinarum*) was a common ingredient, perhaps due to its rarity and also the vaguely humanoid shape of the root. Mandrake is a member of the Solanaceae family, alongside henbane (*Hyoscyamus niger*) and deadly nightshade (*Atropa belladonna*). In *Romeo and Juliet*, Juliet's sleeping potion is laced with mandrake, which perhaps gives us a nefarious indication of why it might be useful in love potions.[63]

Other common ingredients of love potions in England included briony (*Bryonia dioica*) and fern seed. If you want to use the latter, you need to gather it on St John's Eve, but it's worth noting that fern seed doesn't actually exist, as ferns reproduce through spreading spores rather than seed, and the spores don't appear until much later in the year!

Vervain (*Verbena officinalis*) also appears in several recipes, along with animal parts. One medieval recipe told you to grind a dove's heart, sparrow's liver, swallow's womb and hare's kidney into a powder. Then you dried your own blood to a powder and added an equal part to the mixture. This concoction was added to liquid and drunk by your intended.[64]

Italian monk and writer Girolamo Folengo even offered a recipe in the 16th century containing tomb dust, bits of corpses, toad venom, infant's blood, ox bile and other such ingredients.[65] Quite frankly, it sounds more like death metal lyrics than a helpful shopping list, and there's no evidence as to the effects of this formula. It's more likely that these gruesome ingredients actually referred to more mundane items, which had been encoded to prevent the instructions falling into the wrong hands. After all, consider how powerful a love potion that worked would be – you could wreak a lot of havoc.

The biggest problem with a philtre was getting your intended to drink it, especially if it smelled foul. Alternatives did exist, such as rubbing vervain juice into your hands and then touching your intended.[66] Yet that method still involves forcing someone to do something they may not want to do. Perhaps it would be better employed by a couple using the vervain juice on each other as an agreed practice.

Not all love potions involved animal parts or weird and hard-to-source ingredients. One ancient love philtre included three leaves from a red rose (*Rosa*), three leaves from a white rose, three stems of forget-me-not (*Myosotis sylvatica*) and three leaves of speedwell (*Veronica officinalis*).[67] These are all very common plants in Britain, and their symbolism is also notable. In the Victorian language of flowers, red roses meant "love", white roses meant "I am worthy of you", forget-met-nots meant "true love" and speedwell meant "fidelity".[68] (See Chapter 4 for more on plant symbolism.) As the rest of the recipe is not known, you could simply grow these plants in your garden and get the benefit of their symbolism that way.

CHARMS

I know I said earlier that spells and charms replaced philtres in popularity because they were easier to use than a potion, but that didn't necessarily make them any more pleasant to make, and their ingredients weren't always fun. According to the 19th-century poet and folklorist Lady Jane Francesca Wilde, a particularly potent Irish love charm involved a dead body.[69]

The charm instructed a woman to take a piece of skin from the arm of a corpse (whether she needed to raid a grave to source this is not stated). Once she had her corpse skin, she had to tie it to the arm of the person she wanted to love her. It needed to be tied on while the intended partner was asleep, and then removed before they woke up, which sounds like a really weird version of the children's game Buckaroo. Once she'd done this, she had to carefully preserve the skin to retain her lover's ardour.

If that wasn't enough, she could also sleep with the skin strip under her head to dream of her future husband. I'm assuming this latter practice would be done only if there wasn't someone to tie to the skin to, otherwise it could be awkward if she tied the corpse skin to the person she fancied but dreamed of someone entirely different.

Lady Wilde reported that a serving girl tried the "put the skin under your pillow" rite for a laugh, only to find she dreamed of her master. When the lady of the family died, the serving girl remembered her prophetic dream and used the "tie the corpse's skin to the arm" trick on her master. It must have worked because her master married her within the year.

Before you go thinking that it was nice that she got a happy-ever-after out of something so gross, things did not end well for our serving girl. A year and a day after the wedding, a fire broke out in the girl's bedroom, destroying the strip of corpse skin. This broke the charm and turned her husband's inexplicable love for her into hate. Disappointing, yes, but still preferable Tinder, you might say.

Using a charm did not always mean sourcing body parts. This spell involves a spoken charm to discover more about your romantic future. If you were looking for a partner, you were instructed to go to a churchyard and find yarrow (*Achillea millefolium*) growing on a man's grave (if you wanted to find a man) or a woman's grave (if you wanted to find a woman). Pick the yarrow at midnight, saying,

> **"Yarrow, yarrow, I seek thee, yarrow,**
> **and now I have thee found.**
> **I pray to the good Lord Jesus,**
> **as I pluck thee from the ground."**

You would only pull a single stalk and then go home, where you would perform the rest of the spell. Before you got into bed, you would separate the stalk into two sprigs, putting one sprig in your right sock and tying the other to your left leg. Next, you would get into bed backward and say,

**"Good night to thee, yarrow,
Good night to thee, yarrow,
Good night to thee, yarrow."**

Once you were actually in bed, you'd say,

**"Good night, pretty yarrow,
I pray thee, sweet yarrow,
tell me by the morrow,
[and you'd say whatever it was you wanted to know]".**[70]

You could tailor the spell to your question; you didn't just have to use it for love. For example, if you had a legal question, you would find yarrow growing on a judge's grave. If you performed the spell correctly, you would meet the dead spirit from your chosen grave in your dream and they would provide answers while you slept. This is an interesting charm because while you could ask for the name of who you'd marry, you could also request other helpful romantic advice. (We'll talk more about love divination in Chapter 4.)

Spoken charms also appear in divination practices, most likely because they're easy to memorize and there are specific times that you need to use them. Young girls in the rural regions of the southern states of America, for example, used the new moon for fortune telling, especially around love. They looked at the new moon and repeated:

✳ **"New moon, true moon, tell me my fortune,**
Tell me who my true love shall be:
If he be a merchant, let a cock crow;
If he be a farmer, let a cow low;
If he be a soldier, let a horse neigh;
If he be a sailor, let an ass bray;
If he be a teacher, let the sheep-bell ting;
If he be a preacher, let the night-bird sing." ★

Then they listened to see which sound came first to get their answer.[71] Naturally, it would be harder to get this one to work here in the 21st century. There is a far wider range of professions to choose from and you'd be hard pressed to find many of the associated sounds in urban environments, let alone rural ones! You could always tailor it to the most common professions and the sounds you're more likely to hear. At least this charm is broadly positive as it works on the assumption that you will have a future partner. There's no sound that says you won't!

"WHICH WILL YOU TRY?

It's difficult to feel confident in trying these spells because few of their practitioners ever recorded their results. The important thing is that people were so keen to find love that they found magical ways to support their goals – and there's nothing stopping us giving it a go too.

The approaches in this chapter have largely fallen into three categories: spoken word, ritual and the creation of magical items. The folklore practices tend toward spoken word and ritual, requiring everyday items that people might have to hand, or simply the right words in the right order at the right time.

Meanwhile, the more occult practices underline how much wealth played a part in the more formal love magic of earlier times, involving items that were expensive to commission or unpleasant to source (hello, corpse skin?!), or elaborate rituals that were no easy feat to complete. It's somehow comforting that there was a range of folkloric and magical options across varying price points, so at least the quest for love was not solely the preserve of the rich!

Here in the 21st century, we're more likely to tend toward wishes and charms, and if your only ingredients are time, words and the peace and quiet in which to say them, then anyone can get started with love magic.

CHAPTER 3

HOUSEHOLD MAGIC

One of the things you notice when looking at folklore is how often "ordinary" items are used in superstitions, rituals and traditions. It's not really surprising that people would use whatever they had to hand. This might seem strange when you see all the magical accounts on social media today, with their proliferation of beautiful "witchy" items and storebought altarware, but it shows how these practices were once very much in the realm of the everyday. And just as your day is packed with chores and jobs, so our forebears would have needed to save time by finding ways to slot their traditions into their mundane activities.

Thus we end up with household magic! This chapter explores folk practices that involve ordinary household objects, such as candles, food items, clothes and pins, to help identify potential partners or encourage them to make themselves known to the practitioner. Many of these tools and materials remain accessible today – things that you could well have lying around your own home. You'll be able to buy anything you don't already have cheaply at the supermarket or in a charity shop.

✦ BAKED GOODS ✦

In Chapter 1 we talked about food and its involvement in events through the ritual year. Food was a key household item and part of many other traditions, so naturally it was also used in the quest for prophetic dreams of future loved ones. In addition to wedding cake (see page 53), other types of cake served the same purpose.

In England's northern counties, one tradition saw people give fruitcake, gingerbread or Cheshire cheese to new mothers. Yorkshire's version was called pepper-cake and apparently looked like thick gingerbread. This wasn't just a way to celebrate the new mother – it also offered a divinatory possibility to unmarried women. Either the new father or the doctor cut the cake/cheese into chunks and tossed them into the midwife's apron, before handing them to any single girls in the room. Each girl took her chunk home and put it under their pillow to dream of the man she would marry.[72]

Fruitcake or cheese might not immediately seem like obvious foods to connect to love. We are more likely to think of oysters – a famous aphrodisiac – or expensive dinners in fancy restaurants. But people in earlier eras could even look to humble bread.

There was a belief that you could make a loaf known as a "love cake". You rubbed the dough over your body before you baked it, and the inclusion of your sweat would make the person you fancied fall for you. Apparently. A much more pleasant option directed you to make your bread as normal and sit on the oven while it baked. On the one hand, your attractiveness was thought to rise along with the dough. On the other hand, the smell of fresh bread lingering about your person could be equally enticing. This one could certainly be worth giving a go, although for health and safety's sake, I'm pretty sure sitting near the oven is just as helpful as sitting on it.

Alternatively, you could "make cocklebread", which involved climbing onto the table, gathering up your skirts and then wobbling your bum as if you were kneading dough with your buttocks. You'd say "My Dame is sick and gone to bed, and I'll go mould my cocklebread" as you did so.[73] It's not entirely clear what this practice was supposed to do on a practical level. No one knows if the report came from a time when women really did knead bread with their behind, and potentially serve it to their would-be paramour, or if someone told antiquarian John Aubrey about it for a laugh, and he took it seriously.

Even bread and butter could indicate whether you would be married. If you ended up with both bread and butter and cake on your plate, it meant a wedding would happen. It won't necessarily be *your* wedding, but it's worth noting. Before you think it's odd that people might be eating bread and butter and cake at the same time, there is the delightful phenomenon in northern England of the "cakey tea", which includes a buffet of different foodstuffs that might include slices of cake and bread and butter. Alternatively, if a woman took a second piece of bread and butter before she'd finished eating the first piece, she would marry soon.[74] Note: both these circumstances have to come about organically. You can't cheat by doing it on purpose!

To find out which direction your future partner might come from, you need a dog and some poppyseed cake. Break off a piece of cake and throw it out of your front door. Let your dog go to fetch it and pay attention to where it returns from. This is apparently the direction from which your future love will appear. A divination like this makes more sense if you live near a major route bringing people into the place you live.

One practice in Lincolnshire directed women to hide the communion wafer in their mouth at church. They would then go home via a churchyard and spit the wafer at a toad they found there. If the toad ate it, then the man she wanted would be overcome with desire for her.[75] Presumably, if the toad ignored it, then the man she fancied wasn't interested.

FRUIT & VEGETABLES

You could also learn about your love life by counting the seeds in your apple. One meant your lover loved you back. Two meant he didn't. Three meant you'd agree, but four meant he'd forgotten you. Five meant bad luck, while six meant you'd be disappointed in love. Seven meant you'd find a coin and eight meant you'd marry your own choice of partner – clearly this was relevant in earlier centuries when parents would choose their children's partners for strategic reasons. If a man counted eight seeds, however, it meant his beloved would jilt him. Nine seeds told you that you'd get a letter in the next post, while ten meant your love was true.[76] Cutting an appleseed in half when slicing the apple meant your love life would be troubled. Doing this twice meant you'd soon be a widow.[77]

People believed that if a man and a woman shared a beetroot, they'd fall in love. Imagine seeing that in a rom-com.

If a woman didn't know which suitor to choose, she might turn to onions to help her decide. Take as many onions as you have potential partners and carve a name onto each one. Plant them and see which one sprouts first, indicating the person you should favour. [78] You can also apply this method to anything else in life that requires a decision, from holiday destinations to models of car to types of job.

CHEESE

Alternatively, women might practise tyromancy, or divination by cheese, and cut as many blocks of cheese as they had potential partners. They'd carve the names onto each block and whichever one went mouldy first showed them the partner they should choose.[79]

Another way to use tyromancy involved cutting open a blue cheese and looking for initials in the veins. You could no doubt try to read the veins for symbols that might indicate a future spouse's job or even where you might meet them (which, let's be honest, would be the most useful form of divination).

EGGS

Ovomancy, or divination by egg, was also a popular method of love divination. Women might make a Venus glass to find out more information about a future husband. Simply add hot water to a glass, put a small hole in an eggshell and let the whites drip into the water. Pay attention to the shapes made by the egg whites as they solidify.[80] A horse might suggest a farmer, or a fish might indicate a fisherman. This was probably more useful in earlier times when professions had obvious symbols; I'm not sure what shape might indicate a hedge fund manager or a web developer here in the 21st century. In 1956, a woman claimed she had broken an egg into a glass of water at noon on Midsummer's Day and seen a desk in the shapes made by the egg. Sure enough, her husband was a teacher.[81]

In Shropshire, people believed that you would dream of your future partner if you put the first egg laid by a young white hen under your pillow.[82] The superstition doesn't record how you avoided breaking the egg!

In the Ozark Mountains in the US, girls who wanted to know who they would marry would hollow out a hard-boiled egg and fill the hole with salt. They'd eat this before bed and would then dream of their future partner bringing them a bucket of water.[83]

SALT

Speaking of salt, girls in the southern counties of England used salt and a fireplace to bring their lover to them if they hadn't seen them for a while. Every Friday night for three weeks, they threw a pinch of salt into the fire while saying:

> **"It is not this salt I wish to burn,**
> **It is my lover's heart to turn;**
> **That he may neither rest nor happy be**
> **Until he comes and speaks to me."**[84]

Their errant lover would appear on the final night of the ritual. I daresay you could use this charm for a generic "find my true love" option, though finding a functioning fireplace to use every Friday night for three weeks might be more of a hassle than finding a new partner!

DRINKS

In Germany's Harz Mountains, girls followed a specific drinks-related tradition to see a vision of their future husband. They covered their bedroom table with a white cloth and prepared a cup of wine and a cup of water, which they placed on the table. Before bed, they closed their bedroom door, got undressed and repeated a charm:

 **"My dear St Andrew,
Let now appear before me
My heart's beloved.
If he shall be rich,
He will pour a cup of wine;
If he shall be poor,
Let him pour a cup of water."**[85]

If they'd performed the ritual properly, then a vision of their future husband would appear in the room. If he drank from the water, he would  be poor. If he drank from the wine, he would be rich.

 Surprisingly, there is a record of someone trying this tradition and it working. On the stroke of midnight, a man appeared in the girl's room,

took a swig of wine and placed a three-edged knife on the table before he vanished.

Not knowing what else to do with it, the girl hid the knife in a trunk. A few years later, the man she saw in her room arrived in the area to buy property. He met the girl, courted her and then married her. So far, so good, right?

Unfortunately, one day, he needed to fetch something from the trunk, and he spotted the knife. Enraged, he turned on the girl, accusing her of being the woman who forced him to travel so far in the night years before, and stabbed her in the heart with the knife.

There is much here to suggest a cautionary tale against practising such divinations, and the lack of names and dates gives it the feel of an urban legend, but the story does vividly suggest the danger of trying to peer into the future.

 # CANDLES

Candles are perhaps considered a more decorative or luxurious item in the western world in the 21st century, with scented candles bringing a waft of spring or Christmas into the home. Yet, as anyone who keeps a stash of them in case of power cuts knows, they've always had a practical purpose. Candles in earlier centuries would likely have been made from tallow or animal fat, given the cost of beeswax candles. The development of stearin candles in the 1820s and of paraffin candles in the 1850s made this form of lighting more effective and widely available.

In Buckinghamshire, girls would use a candle and two pins to call their lover to them. They took two pins and pushed them through the candle so that the pins went through the wick. While doing this, they recited this charm:

> **"It's not this candle alone I stick,**
> **But [*name*]'s heart I mean to prick;**
> **Whether he be asleep or awake,**
> **I'd have him come to me and speak."**[86]

They lit the candle and waited – legend goes that the lover would pay a visit by the time the candle burned down to the pins (which then caused the flame to go out).

The nurse who reported the charm to folklorist William Henderson knew of three occasions when this spell had been used and each time the lover had made an appearance as intended. One girl was now unhappily married to her lover, but another found herself dumped almost immediately. Her lover had arrived that evening, describing how he had been unable to stay away, but he knew that she'd been up to something and ended their relationship.[87] It just goes to show that using magic to compel another person rarely ends well.

That said, the charm can be adapted to inspire anyone who might have a crush on you to present themselves. Swap out the specific name for "my true love" or "my future partner". You might be tempted to use the smallest candles possible or put the pins near the top of the candle – after all, if they're going to present themselves by the time the flame reaches the candle, then why not hurry things along? But patience is a virtue, so you'd be better off using a taller candle and inserting the pins near the bottom, which gives the person more time to contact you. Burn it in a fireproof container away from drafts and in your presence. Fire safety might not be sexy, but the only sparks you want are between you and your suitor.

In Durham, a variation of this charm saw two people each using a pin to pierce the same candle through the wick. If both pins remained in the wick after the candle burned beyond them, then each person's lover would arrive. If one pin fell out, the lover it represented wasn't faithful. If the pin caused that part of the candle to melt before the flame reached it, then that lover would not arrive, at least that night. In this version, the pins should be stuck into the candle opposite each other.[88]

There was even an option for men. If they found a gate with five bars on it, they were instructed to mark three notches on it every night for nine nights. They would see their sweetheart on the final night.[89] There doesn't appear to have been a spoken charm involved, but perhaps in this case intention was enough.

You can also use candles and pins as a divination if you have several potential partners and you don't know which one to pick. Stick the pins in the candle, naming each pin as the potential suitor. Repeat the above charm, saying "my true love" rather than a specific name, and light the candle. The candle would burn down and the pins would fall out. When the right pin was reached, the door would open and the suitor the pin represented would appear.[90] Again, this demonstrates the value in using candles with long burn times!

BONES

Girls in 19th-century Yorkshire practised a variation on the previous spell that required a sheep's shoulderblade and a penknife, rather than a candle and pins, though the motivation was the same: the girl's partner would be unable to rest until he visited her. One girl in Wakefield reported practicing the charm by piercing the bone from a shoulder of mutton with a brand-new penknife. I've included this in the household magic chapter as you can get hold of bones by buying specific cuts from a butcher. While we don't know exactly which charm the Wakefield girl spoke while doing so, this is the one usually advised for this spell:

> **"'Tis not this bone I mean to stick,**
> **But my lover's heart I mean to prick;**
> **Wishing him neither rest nor sleep**
> **Till he comes to me to speak."**[91]

Our fearless heroine then buried these items, with the knife still stuck in the bone, in the garden. As it turned out, her lover arrived the following day and told her that he'd been experiencing intense feelings of misery since the day before. The girl assumed his misery had begun when she used the spell and while she was convinced that it had worked, she felt so awful for making her lover feel bad that she decided she'd never use it again. It seems the penknife pricked her conscience, as well as his heart.

In another version, an unmarried woman had to repeat the spell every night for nine nights. Each time, she'd pierce the bone with the knife in a different place. The man would then arrive either at the end of nine days, complaining of a wound received during the nine days. He'd ask for something to put on it, giving him an excuse to visit the woman.[92]

An alternative practice from 19th-century Yorkshire saw people using pins and rabbit or sheep shoulderblades to bring on prophetic dreams. They stuck nine pins into the bone and put it under their pillow, before getting into bed backward. Apparently, this was guaranteed to help people dream of the person they fancied, although whether it did or not remains unknown.[93] A rabbit's shoulderblade rather than a sheep's might have been more comfortable to use, if it was going under a pillow. I can't imagine a bone stuck full of pins under your pillow would allow much sleep to happen, let alone any dreaming of crushes!

On the wedding day, it was also important to give the bride the small bone known as a sidesman from a fowl's wing, so she would be happy in her choice of husband.[94] Perhaps that would make a good "something borrowed"!

PINS

Unsurprisingly, you're more likely to encounter the candle and pins version of the "heart-pricking" charm than the penknife and sheep shoulderblade one. Speaking of pins, there were, somewhat unsurprisingly, a range of British superstitions associated with pins and brides. In the 17th century, people believed they needed to throw away the pins used in a bridal gown because it would bring bad luck to the bride if any were left in the dress (this is perhaps rooted in practicality rather than magic). The bridesmaids also had to be careful not to keep any of the pins, or they wouldn't be married before Easter.[95]

By the 19th century, the belief had somewhat changed. Any pins left in the dress after the wedding were believed to be good-luck charms for single women, who would take them in order to marry within the year.[96] Ultimately, the bride needed to get rid of the pins in her dress one way or another, and by 1909 it was believed she must throw them either over the left shoulder or into the fire for luck.[97] A 1950s belief also claimed that anyone who wore a pin used to make a bridal gown would marry within the year. In the 1960s, the *Folklore* journal reported that one dressmaker gave the pins used for wedding dresses to her friends to help them pick out the names of racehorses to bet on![98]

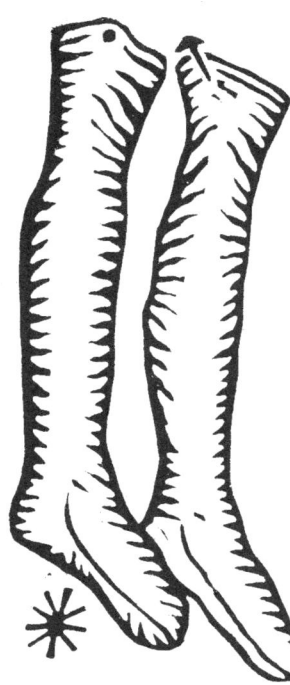

People carrying pins with them will never marry, and apparently neither will men who hold their clothes together with safety pins.[99] I can't help thinking that this one might have been put about by tailors hoping to entice men to have their clothes repaired. It wasn't just dressmaking pins you had to worry about, either. Losing a hairpin meant you'd be crossed in love or that someone you loved was thinking about you. Those inconsistencies, eh?[100]

There was even a simple charm involving your stockings and a pin, which resembles the candle spell. Girls in the early 20th century in England might pin their stockings to the wall and say,

"I hang my stocking on the wall,
Hoping my true love to call;
May he neither rest, sleep, nor happy be,
Until he comes and speaks to me."[101]

There is no guidance as to when this spell should be done, nor does it require a pre-existing partner. You could combine it with other charms in this chapter and perform it on nine consecutive nights, or try it out on a Friday, the day ruled by Venus.

Finally, pins were important in another class of charm, which involved sticking them in an animal's heart. A 19th-century charm from Leeds suggested killing a pigeon, removing its heart and sticking pins in it. The girl was to put this under her pillow and, as with the pins-in-the-shoulderblade rite, go backward into bed. If she did this, she'd dream of her future husband.

Somewhat worryingly, this is not the only recorded use of pins and an animal heart. In 1904, a sexton in Lincolnshire discovered a woman had buried a hare's heart, stuck with 385 pins. Burying such a heart near a new grave would impact the health of a faithless lover, who would die when the heart completely decayed.

This echoes a recorded witchcraft practice in which a witch confessed she had sought to kill a young woman by sticking a heart made of wax with pins. Women in Lincolnshire were later advised to stick a pigeon's heart with pins to force their crush to marry them, whether he wanted to or not. This seems very different from the earlier practice of sticking pins into a hare's heart to punish a faithless lover and shows how traditions change over time.[102]

✹ CLOTHES ✦

In Chapter 1, we looked at the 19th-century practice of putting your shoes at right angles before going to bed, to induce a dream of a partner.[103] One version from Jersey involved putting your boots on the floor under your bed, forming a T directly beneath your pillow. Once in bed, you'd say,

> ✳ **"I've put my shoes in the form of a T,**
> **Hoping my true love to see,**
> **Let him be young or let him be old,**
> **Let him come and visit me."[104]**

Girls could also use their stockings for divination. They would pull the left stocking into the right, saying,

> ✳ **"This is the blessed Friday night;**
> **I draw my left stocking into my right,**
> **To dream of the living, not of the dead,**
> **To dream of the young man I am to wed."**

Then she wouldn't speak to anyone for the rest of the night, and go to bed.[105] In Northumberland, girls would tie their left stocking around their neck to dream of their future husband, which has somewhat disturbing connotations.

Girls could also see an image of their true love using a corset-based divination. Upon going to bed, they removed their corset, rolled it up and repeated this charm three times:

"I roll it, oh roll it, ah roll it up tight,
And hope that my true love I'll see in the night.
Not in his coffin and not in his clay
But in the good clothes that he wears every day."[106]

The corset continues a tradition of dream symbolism, where girdles were believed to foretell the future. Dreaming of a girdle signified a successful marriage, a broken one warned of danger and an old, worn girdle suggested trouble ahead. A golden girdle meant wealth, a silver one meant loss and a copper one meant happiness.[107]

Keeping a hat on the table meant you were disappointed, while sitting on your hat meant you were in love.[108] Losing your underwear apparently meant your partner loved someone else.[109] In the west of England, if an unmarried woman's garter loosened while she was out walking, it meant her sweetheart was thinking of her. Yet in Yorkshire, if her garter fell off and she lost it in the street, her sweetheart was unfaithful.[110]

THE LANGUAGE OF THE GLOVE

If you've ever watched a costume drama, you've probably gotten frustrated that female characters rarely tell male characters how they feel thanks to the social conventions that prevented anyone from being "forward". The characters have to either drop hints or rely on facial expressions or body language to let someone know they're interested.

Somewhat unsurprisingly, therefore, there was an entire language involved with what you did with your gloves that related to flirting and romance, which was used in those earlier times when it was deemed uncouth to express yourself. Now, this language has its own issues, because if everyone knew what a gesture meant, then anyone looking at you could still follow your meaning. That's probably why twirling your gloves around the fingers meant "We are watched".

So what other gestures might you make? You could say "I love you" by dropping both gloves. If you pulled the glove halfway onto your left hand, it meant "indifference". Be careful though: having the left glove halfway on but with the thumb exposed asked the other person if they loved you. The same position on the right hand meant "Kiss me".

Striking the glove on the hand meant "I am shocked", while biting the tips meant "I wish to be rid of you". Turning them inside out meant "I hate you", and putting the gloves away meant "I am vexed". Clenching a glove and rolling it up meant either yes or no – the right glove for no, the left for yes.

Striking your glove over your shoulder invited the other to follow you, though striking the chin meant you loved another. Using the gloves as a fan meant "Introduce me to your company", but carefully folding them up meant "Get rid of company".

It would be interesting to know how often people actually used the language of gloves. Was it like the language of flowers, which may have been a cool idea but seems to have been rarely practiced? If nothing else, you can teach your friends what the gestures mean and try them out in noisy pubs.

TEXTILE & KNOT MAGIC

While dressmaking has enjoyed a welcome resurgence in recent years, textile lore would have had more significance in the past when sewing materials would have been common household items. Finding a piece of red fabric, especially if it was wool, meant luck in love.[111] Finding new ribbon, string or silk meant you'd be successful in love.[112] Meanwhile, finding a darning needle meant you'd be disappointed in love.[113] I find this one fascinating, since darning usually means repairing something and making it usable again. Surely that should be a sign that you'd be good at conflict resolution?

Given we've just mentioned string, it seems only right to discuss knot magic in relation to love. In *Daemonologie* (1597), his bizarre treatise on witchcraft, James I of England and VI of Scotland accused couples of tying knots on their wedding day in order to stay married – and today we still refer to marriage as "tying the knot". This type of magic was accessible to ordinary people, and you don't even need to be particularly crafty to do it.

Knot magic involves tying knots into ribbon, string or thread, the idea being that the knot "holds" whatever intention you have while tying the knot. It appears in folklore as the belief that witches could recite charms to raise the wind and "tie" it into a knot. Sailors could then buy these to release the wind if sailing conditions weren't favourable. People could also tie positive or protective qualities into their knots, which explains why knot magic was popularly used to ward off illness and death, to aid love and childbirth and to protect against demons.[114]

One love charm involving knots had to be performed by men. In 19th-century Glamorganshire, a man might steal a girl's garters and weave them into a lover's knot while speaking words of love in Welsh. He had to wear the knot under his shirt until bedtime, at which point he put it under his pillow. If he'd done it all correctly, he would dream of his future wife. A similar charm was recorded in Newcastle in 1899, but it's not specified if it's aimed at women or men. The person performing the charm needed to make nine tight knots in their garter and this would bring on prophetic dreams of their future partner.[115]

You could also use knots to find out if someone loved you. If something became tangled into a knot and you couldn't undo it, then you simply said a person's name. If they loved you, the knot would untie.[116]

One ancient Greek love spell requires you to make a thread from hemp and red wool, and then tie 14 knots into it, reciting a magic spell with each knot. Then tie this cord around your waist and it will attract a lover.[117] This shows the main advantage of knot magic – people could tie and carry knots without anyone knowing. Indeed, you could even use knot magic on your shoelaces when you tie them!

You could try an updated version of the Greek spell above using ribbons, yarn or cords in colours you associate with love. Seven or nine knots could be a good option, given how prevalent both numbers are in folklore all over the world. Visualize yourself attracting and retaining the kind of love that you want and "knot" that image into the ribbon or cord. You could carry it with you, perhaps adding an appropriate pendant and wearing it around your neck if it's long enough. If your pendant is copper, a metal associated with Venus, then that would bring you some extra magical bang for your buck!

Speaking of Venus, Classical myth also provides us with the Girdle of Aphrodite, later known as the Girdle of Venus. No one is entirely sure what it looked like, since the first mention of it in Book 14 of Homer's *Iliad* is scant on details. All he says is that Hera wanted to seduce her husband Zeus and, having dressed in her finery, asked Aphrodite for love and desire. Aphrodite undid an embroidered band from around her chest, woven with love, desire and beguilement, and handed it to Hera, advising her to put it on. Aphrodite also promised Hera that she would accomplish whatever she desired, so the goddess of love was clearly pretty confident in her girdle's power.

The story of Juno, the Roman equivalent of Hera, borrowing the girdle from Venus, the Roman version of Aphrodite, appeared in 18th-century art alongside other Classical themes (most likely because it meant artists got to paint half-naked women). Various theories have been put forward as to what the girdle looked like. But whatever it was, the gods believed it made them irresistible. Clearly, mortals aren't going to be able to lay their hands on the Girdle of Aphrodite. Yet you could use knot magic to make your own equivalent of the magical girdle, perhaps using macrame to weave love and affection into your creation.

MIRRORS

For centuries, mirrors have been employed to divine the future through the practice of scrying, and I have no doubt that before mirrors became widely affordable, still ponds or lakes were used as a reflective surface. As I mentioned in Chapter 1, I remember reading in teenage magazines back in the 1990s about Hallowe'en practices involving gazing into a mirror after sunset while either brushing your hair or eating an apple. With any luck, you'd see a vision of your future partner reflected in the mirror. I'll be honest, it never worked for me as a teenager, and I tried it again last Hallowe'en and the only thing that happened was that I felt very silly. My hair did look immaculate after all that brushing though.

Mirrors with the power to tell you about love appear in various legends, which shows us just how much humans would love to be able to take a peek into one and find the truth about a romantic situation. In "The Squire's Tale" in *The Canterbury Tales*, Chaucer relates how the King of Arabia sends a magic mirror to Cambuscan, the King of Tartary (sometimes identified with Genghis Khan), for his birthday. It could show the viewer all sorts of useful things, such as who was a true friend and who was a foe, and it could also reveal if the person you loved was true to you. The King of Arabia also sends a brass horse that can take the rider wherever he wants in the world in a day, a sword that will cut through any armour and cause a wound that will never heal (unless the bearer of the sword touches the wound with the flat blade), and a ring that will let the wearer speak with animals and know the properties of all herbs[118] – which puts an Amazon gift voucher somewhat to shame.

But why would mirrors be relevant to love magic and divination? English folklore might provide a possible explanation in the belief that the mirror reflected the soul. After all, people covered the mirrors in the home of someone who had died so their soul wouldn't become trapped in the mirror and be unable to leave the house altogether. Some were so afraid of this that they even covered mirrors in sickrooms.[119] If you're looking for your soulmate, then it stands to reason that you might turn to the very item that reveals the soul.

You might want to try some basic mirror scrying. Some people stare at their own reflection until they start to see images in the mirror. Others watch the reflection of flames. Anything to relax the mind to the point where images and symbols begin to appear in the mirror. I've recently seen this described on American ghost-hunting television programmes as "dark magic", with people confidently asserting that a mirror is a "portal", but I have yet to find a ghost story in which a being came *out* of a mirror. If it does worry you, you can always use still water instead, which makes an excellent scrying surface.

If you do want to try mirror scrying, make a special divinatory mirror that you use for nothing else. The most common method involves leaving a mirror out under moonlight overnight. Sprinkle a magical infusion of cold mugwort tea over the surface and let it dry. Mugwort (*Artemisia vulgaris*) is a herb traditionally used to help boost psychic powers. You might ask something like, "What does my love life hold?", and gaze into the mirror. See if any images or symbols appear in the glass, and then work out how these images provide an answer. You might not see anything obvious in the mirror, but you might see pictures in your head or get ideas as subtle sensations. If you don't see or sense anything at first, don't lose heart. Keep practising! You might use this practice for something tangible, such as asking what you might wear on a date, or where you might go to meet someone. Whatever you choose, keep your scrying mirror covered when not in use.

There is little in folklore specifically about using mirrors to make magic, no doubt due to the relative scarcity of mirrors when much folklore was collected. That said, you can find variations on a simple glamour spell involving a mirror, and if you're looking to meet a new partner, feeling glamorous and confident might be the boost you're after. Get yourself in front of a mirror – any mirror. Instead of focusing on how you actually look in the reflection, visualize how you want to be seen. While visualizing that, see yourself bathed in a golden light. Once you feel completely confident, go on with your day!

'WHICH WILL YOU TRY?

Naturally, some household magic spells are easier to do than others, depending on what you have in your home. People are probably less likely to have bones lying around, but many food items are still common, or at least easily substituted. The everyday nature of many of these items also shows how easily magical practice could be concealed from prying eyes. Are you cutting up an apple for a snack, or divining the future? Only you would know! The fact that many of these practices slot into ordinary household tasks, the daily rituals of making meals and getting ready for bed, etc., demonstrates that magic was not necessarily considered something that required a lot of equipment or experience. That many of these traditions relate to stereotypically female occupations – cooking, textile crafts, preparing food, mending – also returns us to the idea that the search for love was primarily undertaken by women. Or at least that their traditions were the ones that were recorded.

What I love about these practices is that they are so tightly woven into the everyday that they show us how mundane and even normalized magic might be – which certainly supports the idea that it's possible to live an enchanted life in the 21st century, too.

CHAPTER 4

WORKING with PLANTS

Most youngsters have dabbled with plant divination at some point, plucking petals from flowers to find out if somebody loves them. If you're from the same generation as me, you no doubt made your own "perfume" by soaking petals in water (for me, it was always roses). While it's unlikely that such a scent would last long, it shows our association between plants and smelling good. It's also unlikely that Little You knew you were engaging with a long tradition of using plants to attract love or divine the future!

In this chapter we're going to explore how to work with plants to attract a partner, tell our romantic fortune or send messages of love. We'll look at trees as well because they are easy to identify. Some plant practices were linked to a particular day or time of year, as we discussed in Chapter 1, but many could be done whenever the plant or tree involved was in flower. Lots of the flowers originally used for divination are now declining or rare in the wild, so unless a plant is very abundant it is best to buy it from a supermarket, florist or garden centre, or grow them yourself, to provide a sustainable source for your love magic and divination throughout the year.

The practices in this chapter don't take the animist approach that so many are turning to today, which sees plants and trees as individuals with their own spirits. If that resonates with you, you might wish to befriend these gentle beings before you ask for their help.

GROWING PLANTS

It's beyond the scope of this book to define magic, yet the idea of taking specific actions to achieve a desired result is common to the practices in this chapter. These are not "spells", but rather actions that people believed would bring them love, whether that's carrying a particular plant or growing it. Some practices are more passive than others, but they all relate to plants or trees.

If you're green-fingered, you might like to know that growing your own plants was believed to be an easy way to invite love into your life. At the very least, plants make any space a happier and calmer place to spend time. While lemon balm (*Melissa officinalis*) is most often associated with boosting memory and uplifting the mood, growing and tending the plant was also believed to attract a gentle partner.[120] As it's part of the vigorous mint family, lemon balm is easy to grow and you can also make delicious tea from its leaves, so it might be worth a try.

If you don't fancy growing lemon balm, perhaps because of its tendency to take over a garden, then consider sea aster (*Aster tripolium*)[121] or vervain (*Verbena officinalis*)[122] instead to invite love into your life. Sea aster could also ward off evil spirits, which seems like a helpful bonus – maybe it deters would-be partners who don't have your best interests at heart![121] Planting pansies (*Viola tricolor*) in the garden in the shape of a heart was also believed to call in love as well as act as a form of divination – if the plants grew, you knew love would likewise grow.

Spring crocuses (*Crocus vernus*) are a good gardening option to attract love, and the range of origin myths associated with the plant might help to explain why. In the most common version of the story, Crocus was a human youth who started a relationship with a nymph named Smilax. He became unhappy with the relationship and the gods enabled him to escape it by turning him into a plant. For some reason, they turned Smilax into a yew tree, which seems a little unfair on Smilax.

In another version, Crocus sought permission to marry Smilax, but the gods refused. Distraught, Crocus killed himself, and out of pity Flora, the goddess of flowers, turned both him and Smilax into plants.

A different version places Crocus as the companion of the god Hermes. An innocent game went wrong when Hermes accidentally killed Crocus with a discus. Distraught by what happened, Hermes turned him into a flower, though whether this was to conceal the evidence or to honour Crocus is unclear.

Yet another version of the myth claims Zeus and Hera were enjoying each other's company so passionately that the river bank they lay on erupted with crocus flowers, and the crocus has been associated with love ever since. The fact they start to bloom in February, near Valentine's Day, probably helps, and in some sources, the crocus was even dedicated to St Valentine. You can see why growing it in your garden was believed to help attract love into your life, although I can't help thinking the Zeus and Hera option is the more positive version of the story!

If you don't have a garden, growing thyme (*Thymus vulgaris*) as a houseplant can act as a miniature altar to Venus, because the plant is sacred to the goddess, and will also help bring you courage in love.[123]

WEARING PLANTS

Thyme is available in most supermarkets, so an easy way to make yourself irresistible is to tuck a sprig into your hair.

Wearing sprigs of other plants was also believed to help in attracting love. Aster (*Callistephus chinensis*) was a good choice, as was camphire, also known as henna (*Lawsonia inermis*). The pansy (*Viola tricolor*) was an excellent option, and yerba mate (*Ilex paraguariensis*) would also attract someone of the opposite sex to you.

If you wore fresh endive (*Cichorium endivia*), you needed to replace it every three days for it to continue to work its magic. Lady's bedstraw (*Galium verum*) was another option, while you could wear betony (*Stachys officinalis*) if you were ready to approach someone you had a crush on.

This practice of wearing flowers wasn't just aimed at women, either. Men in love would wear cornflowers (*Centaurea cyanus*) as a buttonhole. If it faded quickly, it meant his intended didn't return his love. This helps to explain why the flowers are also known as bachelor's buttons.

In the Swiss Alps, if you wanted someone to fall in love with you, then you needed to find the black vanilla orchid (*Orchis nigritella*). Slipping it under a boy's pillow or into a girl's apron pocket caused them to fall head over heels for you.[124] In a much more ethical version, in the west of England, a girl might wear a sprig of red valerian (*Centranthus ruber*), today a popular garden plant, to make sure she never lacked partners.[125] This attraction ritual was less subtle than some of them: if people knew what red valerian signified, it would clearly advertise you were available and looking!

If you were worried that wearing a sprig might give away your intentions and you wanted something more discreet (or you just didn't have anywhere to pin it), you could also carry a small pouch of columbine (*Aquilegia*) seeds, lemon balm (*Melissa officinalis*) leaves or liquorice (*Glycyrrhiza glabra*) root for the same purpose. If you wanted to make an amulet to attract love, then putting a bayberry (*Myrica*) leaf in it would help.

A young man who was going to a dance and hoped to attract a partner would look for the poisonous cuckoopint (*Arum maculatum*) on his way there. He'd put a piece of the plant in his shoe and it would attract girls to him. The charm supposedly brought him the prettiest dance partners, though that's presumably based only on his perception of prettiness.[126] The use of cuckoopint in this practice shouldn't be lost on us given the phallic nature of the spadix – the part of the plant that sticks out of the leaves and attracts flies which help to pollinate it. The name cuckoopint gives away its phallic connotations. "Pint" (pronounced to rhyme with "mint") comes from the Old English word for penis, so we can imagine what a young chap looking for this plant was hoping to do with his dance partners.

USING SCENT

Other methods for attracting love were relatively simple and didn't involve growing plants or wearing them. Adding an infusion of chamomile (*Anthemis nobilis*) or lovage (*Levisticum officinale*) to your bath was believed to help, especially if you were meeting new people. Lovage in particular was thought to make you more attractive. Scenting your clothes with the flowers of lavender (*Lavandula angustifolia*), a plant that has long been associated with love and romance, also helped in the quest for a partner. This explains the famous rhyme:

**"Lavender's green, dilly dilly, Lavender's blue,
You must love me, dilly dilly, 'cause I love you."**

If you want to write your crush a love note, then do so using beetroot juice. If you scent the paper with lavender too, then even better! And if you don't have a crush but you just want to invite a partner into your life, you could tie a single strand of your hair to a wild cherry tree. I've tried the last option every year for the last three years, but as yet nothing has happened. Hope springs eternal!

DREAM DIVINATION

As we saw in Chapter 1, girls used to drink lavender tea to ask St Luke to show them who they might marry. Other plants were also used to induce prophetic dreams that would reveal the occupation of a future partner, or even just provide confirmation that the dreamer would find someone. Dreaming of red roses (*Rosa*) was considered a sign of success in love and good luck in general.[127] Dreaming about clover (*Trifolium*) meant you'd have a happy marriage.[128]

On Guernsey, girls sought two fronds of agrimony (*Agrimonia eupatoria*) with nine leaves on each frond, in order to dream of their future husband. They'd place the fronds across each other, securing them in the cross shape with two new pins, and then put the charm under their pillow.[129] Pins play an important role in folk rituals as we saw in Chapter 3, so combining them with plants as in this ritual gives an added punch of magic.

In northern England, one custom directed young women to put ash leaves under their pillow if they wanted to dream of their future husband.[130] There is no specific date associated with this one, so I would suggest trying it on a Friday, the day ruled by Venus, and ideally during a new or waxing moon.

A FORM OF MINDFULNESS

There are many ways of working with plants in a divinatory sense, beyond using them to encourage dreams of the future. Most of us will have picked a daisy and pulled off its petals, to see if the final one tells us "he/she loves me" or "he/she loves me not". The divinatory aspect of plants is also expressed through flower omens – for example, seeing a red rose bloom in autumn in Scotland meant a wedding was on the way, though it wasn't necessarily going to be *your* wedding.[131]

As they went about their day, young women were advised to keep an eye out for an "even ash", which was an ash (*Fraxinus excelsior*) leaf with the leaflet missing from the end, leaving an equal number of leaflets down each side. If they found one, they should put it into their glove, saying,

**"The even ash in my glove,
The first I meet shall be my love."[132]**

Then they needed to pay attention to who they encountered first while carrying the ash in their glove, though the custom doesn't say what would happen if the person turned out to be married or – worse – a close relative!

An alternative version sought to address this problem. It specified looking for an ash leaf with nine leaflets. When you found one, you pressed it to your chest and said,

✦ **"Here's an ash leaf with nine leaves on.**
Take it and press it to your heart
And the first chap you meet'll be your sweetheart.
If he's married let him pass by. ✦
If he's single, let him draw nigh."[133]

A similar practice involves clover (*Trifolium repens*). Normally, we only hear about clover when it's the four-leaf variety. Yet finding a two-leaf clover was also a helpful sign if you sought a partner. You'd pick the clover and hide it in your right shoe before going on your way. It was important to stay focused because the first young man you met would either be your future partner or would have the same name as your future partner.[134]

These practices involving ash and clover highlight one of the central aspects of divination – getting us to pay attention to the world around us. Many of these love divinations are a form of mindfulness, suggesting that we remain present and watch out for anything of note, which, if you're looking for a partner, means you're more aware of potential lovers than if you walk around with your head in the clouds.

'WHO TO CHOOSE?

If you were lucky enough to have a series of potential partners in mind and you wanted to know which one to choose, divination could help there, too. Girls would make a tisty-tosty, a ball made from cowslip (*Primula veris*). Together, they would pick 50–60 cowslip flowerheads and hang them on a string, pushing the flowers together and pulling the string tight to create the ball. They then gathered in a circle and tossed the tisty-tosty between them, saying out loud the names of potential partners as they did so. Whichever name was being spoken at the moment someone dropped the ball was "the one".[135]

Girls also used thistles (*Cirsium vulgare*) to find which of her beaus loved her best. She would cut as many thistle heads as she had suitors, name each head for a suitor and put them all under her pillow. The suitor that loved her most would put out a fresh shoot by morning.[136]

I find it somewhat ironic that you'd use a plant as prickly as a thistle in a love divination, but given the tenacity of thistles and their protective qualities, it's possible that this one works to identify the partner you don't need to protect yourself against. It weeds out the wrong ones by showing you the right one. Of course, the tradition doesn't tell you what to do if none of them shows a fresh shoot, which is one of the downsides of these practices. They assume something will happen and if it doesn't, the poor girl is left to draw the conclusion that she has no intended beloved. If you try a divination like this one and nothing happens, don't worry. Just assume that it didn't work because you haven't met the right person yet.

Luckily, our next charm has a failsafe positive built into it. Girls with several prospective husbands could use hazelnuts to identify the right candidate. (It is fascinating how many of these practices assumed that girls might have several suitors to choose from, which gives me hope that they were marrying men they liked, rather than settling for someone because they had to.) The girls assigned the names of potential matches to different hazelnuts and tossed the nuts into the fire. Whichever nut gave the loudest pop or brightest flame indicated the best prospect.[137] At least one of them was bound to go "pop", and if all of them popped, you could still identify the loudest one.

If you only have chestnuts to hand, fear not! You can use those too. Name each nut after a suitor and put them in front of an open fire. Activate the divination by saying,

**"Maidens, name your chestnuts true
The first to burst belongs to you!"**

Whichever partner you should pick will be the one to burst first.[138]

You could also do this with apple pips, again if you're lucky enough to have several suitors as well as access to an open fire. Collect as many apple pips as you have potential partners. The charm directs you to say,

**"If you love me, pop and fly
If you hate me, lay and die."[139]**

Then toss the pips into the fire. It doesn't specify how you do this, but I'd be inclined to throw them one at a time so you can keep track of which pip is which partner. If you throw them all in at once, it'll be impossible to remember. Besides, it would be a really unhelpful result if you threw them all in and they all popped at once!

A more straightforward option just requires the pips and your own face. Assign different apple pips to different partners, and then press the pips to your cheek or forehead. The ones that stick love you, while the ones that fall off have no regard for you.[140]

These kinds of divinations can also be used for other decisions if you change what the pips represent.

"WILL YOU END UP TOGETHER?

Sometimes, you might have someone in your life that you love, but you're not sure if you'll end up together. You may not know if they even like you in a romantic sense. While I would advise you simply to tell them and give them the opportunity to let you know how they feel, that's far too humdrum an approach for folklore. After all, folklore would advise you to pull petals off a daisy to find out your answer. But perhaps you'd like a real challenge! Try turning a bluebell (*Hyacinthoides non-scripta*) inside out without tearing it. If you manage it, you'll win the one you love.

If you were in Suffolk and you wanted to know if the person you liked also liked you, you could find and pluck some yarrow (*Achillea millefolium*), while saying,

"Green yarrow, green yarrow, you bears a white blow
If my love loves me, my nose will bleed now!"[141]

Nothing says "true love" like an impromptu nosebleed.

Another way of discovering if someone returned your feelings was to pluck a sprig of witch's hair (*Cuscuta*), then ask if your loved one loved you while throwing the sprig over your shoulder at the plant. You left the plant and returned the next day. If the sprig had reattached itself, it meant your intended returned your love. If not, then they didn't.

If a girl had a boy trying to win her affections, she could use plant divination to test his mettle. She'd pluck orpine (*Sedum telephium*) and tuck it into the cracks around his door on Midsummer's Eve. Then she'd come back the next day to see what his real intentions were. If the plant leaned to the right, he would be true. To the left, and he'd lie to her.[142]

There was a divination aimed at boys, too. If they wanted to know if they stood a chance with a girl, they would prick her initials on a laurel (*Laurus nobilis*) leaf, then put it under their cap. They would examine it later, and if the letters had turned red, the girl would return their affections.[143]

Primroses (*Primula vulgaris*) were also part of a love divination aimed at both girls and boys. If someone wanted to know if they would find happiness with their sweetheart, they had to pick a primrose flower and cut the tops of the stamens off. Then they had to hide the flower and think about their sweetheart for the rest of that day and night. If, the next day, the stamens had grown back to their previous height, the relationship would go well. If not, they would be disappointed.[144]

DIVINING INFORMATION ABOUT A FUTURE PARTNER

People often wanted to know a little something about their future partner, such as their job or where they came from. An easy plant divination to tell you the latter involves the humble apple pip again. Hold it with your forefinger and thumb. Squeeze it while saying,

> **"Kernel, come kernel, hop over my thumb,**
> **And tell me which way my true love will come,**
> **East, west, north or south,**
> **Kernel jump into my true love's mouth."**[145]

When it pops out between your finger and thumb, pay attention to the direction it flies in. You might need to use the compass app on your smartphone. As with the similar poppyseed cake ritual in Chapter 3, it's up to you if you want to take the answer as the literal direction from which someone might come to your door or a more general indication as to where in the world they come from.

A different practice directed young women to head to the nearest graveyard and find yarrow growing on a young man's grave. She needed to pluck some of the plant, sew it into a small flannel sachet and put the sachet under her pillow while saying,

✱

**"Yarrow, sweet yarrow, the first that I have found,
And in the name of Jesus, I pluck it from the ground.
As Joseph loves sweet Mary and took her for his dear,
So in a dream this very night my true love will appear!"[146]** ✱

Yarrow is famous for its tiny flowerheads and feathery leaves, so sewing it up in flannel (as in the fabric called flannel, not the washcloth referred to as a flannel) would help keep the plant together. Finding the plant on a young man's grave must have added to the symbolism of the ritual if you yourself were looking for a young man. The charm doesn't explicitly say that you're calling on the deceased young man for his help, but the mention of a grave suggests this was part of the charm.

In 1700s Scotland, you might "pull the kale" to find out more about your future spouse. A person would wear a blindfold and wander through a kale (*Brassica oleracea*) field at midnight and then pull up the first bunch of leaves they stumbled across. The size and shape of the kale stalks suggested the physique your partner would have, while the taste of the kale indicated their temperament. For example, bitter kale meant someone with a bitter personality, while a long, sturdy stalk indicated a tall, strong person.

Even the amount of dirt on the stalk revealed how much money your spouse would have: a clean stalk indicated poverty, whereas a stalk covered in earth meant wealth. Poet Robert Burns mentioned the practice in his 1785 poem "Halloween", in which a disappointed character pulls a kale root with a curl like a pig's tail in it. While Burns is not explicit about what that meant, it does suggest a less-than-hoped-for physique in a future partner. This is a fascinating practice because it was open to both men and women and reveals that men would be just as likely as women to want to know who they would marry.

Other charms enabled you to find out your future partner's initials. One superstition related to gathering wildflowers, claiming the flowers you picked would reveal your husband-to-be's initials. So picking crocus (*Crocus vernus*), anemone (*Anemone coronaria*) and eyebright (*Euphrasia officinalis*) would yield a spouse with the initials C.A.E.[147] This one is open to manipulation, of course, as you could intentionally pick flowers with the initials you wanted. It also depends on the season and which plants happen to be flowering. In any case, picking wildflowers today is a no-no, and in many places you might only be able to find dandelions and daisies!

Instead, try heading to a garden centre or florist. Quietly set the intention that you'll discover the initials of your future partner, or ask your favourite love deity for guidance if you work with one. Close your eyes, count to three and then open them again. Note the first two or three flowers you see and the order in which you notice them. This will give the initials you're looking for!

I tried this one by standing at the back door of my house, closing my eyes and counting to three. When I opened them, I kept my gaze as unfocused as possible and noted the first three plants that grabbed my attention. I saw crososmia (*Crocosmia*), then rhubarb (*Rheum rhabarbarum*) and lavender (*Lavandula angustifolia*), which gave me the initials C.R.L.

I also tried a digital version and simply put "summer flowers UK" into Google Images. The first three results were larkspur (*Delphinium*), African daisies (*Osteospermum*) and sunflowers (*Helianthus annuus*). So I'd be looking for the initials L.A.S.

It goes without saying that you probably shouldn't do this more than once or you'll get similarly mixed messages, although if you did it three times in different places and got the same letters every time, that would be worth paying attention to.

This practice could also be helpful if you have several beaux to choose from, helping you narrow it down. I'll leave it up to you whether you want to use the common name or the botanical name of the plants. After all, many plants have several common names, so you may have to decide which one to use. If I use the botanical names for the first three plants thrown up by the search engine divination, then the initials become D.O.H.! (The irony is not lost on me. How very "Homer Simpson" of Google.)

Apples turn up yet again in this very easy method to find out your future partner's first initial. Simply recite the alphabet while twisting the apple stalk. Whichever letter you get to when the stalk comes away is the initial of your partner's name. Every time I've tried this, and I've done it multiple times, I never get past the letter "G", which doesn't bode well for anyone whose initial lies in the latter half of the alphabet. A slightly different option gives you the opportunity to find out the initial of his surname as well. Do the "stalk twisting" method to get the first initial. Then, recite the alphabet again while tapping the apple with the now-removed stalk. The letter you reach once the stalk pierces the skin will be the initial of his surname.[148]

The second method is much more tricky as you need to peel an apple in a continuous length – you've probably seen this one touted as a divination practice for Hallowe'en, but nothing is stopping you from trying this whenever you want. Once you get the whole peel off the apple, either toss it over your shoulder or hang it from a nail in the door (if you don't have a nail, then a coat peg should do). The peel should form a letter, which will give you the initial of your future partner. With this practice, I always feel sorry for anyone whose name begins with letters like K, Q, W or X![149]

Not everyone wanted the specifics of who they would marry; they just wanted reassurance they would get to marry at all. In Lower Saxony, girls put sprigs of St John's wort (*Hypericum perforatum*) at the head of the bed or hung it on their walls on St John's Eve. If it was fresh the next day, they'd marry within the year. If it drooped, they would not. At least the charm could only predict one year ahead, so if your sprig drooped you could always try again the following St John's Eve.

Our last plant divinatory practice straddles the line between divination and magic because it aims to conjure a vision of your future spouse. It required two girls and some herb-Paris (*Paris quadrifolia*) leaves (another plant now becoming uncommon, so don't pick it in the wild). Each girl sat alone in a room in silence between midnight and 1am. During this hour, she pulled from her head the number of hairs that matched her age and put them in a linen cloth with the leaves. At 1am, she burned them, one at a time, saying,

"I offer this my sacrifice,
To him most precious in my eyes,
I charge thee now come forth to me;
That I this minute may thee see."[150]

If the charm worked, a vision of her future husband would appear and walk around her before disappearing. The use of her own hair makes this more like a spell than a simple divination, as it ties the practitioner into the summoning of the vision. If no one appeared, presumably you would assume there was to be no husband for you.

SENDING MESSAGES WITH PLANTS

Many of the practices described above are aimed at girls, but making symbolic gestures with plants was something that the boys could do in the pursuit of love. If a boy gave a girl a birch twig, it meant his love was constant.[151]

However, the messages weren't always positive ones. In Wales, boys might signify they'd changed their mind or wanted to break an engagement by giving a girl a hazel stick.[152] Presumably they handed the stick over, rather than simply leaving it by her door. Young men wore willow wreaths if they'd been unlucky in courtship.[153] This suggests they wanted to let people know they were feeling vulnerable without having to say so.

The Victorian language of flowers is perhaps the most famous system of sending messages through plants. I have seen it described as a "secret" language, but I'd dispute this. After all, if people could access lists of flower meanings, it would hardly have been difficult to decode the message, but it did allow people to communicate something without saying it aloud or in writing – "restraint" is a theme with the Victorians.

Floriography, which is more of a set of gestures than an actual "language", can still be used today. Granted, your recipient

might not understand your message, but that needn't stop you from being thoughtful.

A key figure in the development of floriography was Lady Mary Wortley Montagu, the wife of the British ambassador in Turkey. In the early 1700s, she wrote letters home about the practice of *selam*, in which she described harem ladies using flowers to pass secret messages to their lovers, as written ones could be intercepted.[154]

Many have since noted that *selam* was a rhyming game, not a secret flower language, so Montagu either misunderstood it or deliberately romanticized it for her readers. Either way, she spoke over the people who actually practiced it. History – and folklore – is littered with examples of a good story being preferred to the truth! Still, the publication of her embassy letters caught the public imagination and people seized on the idea of sending messages using flowers.

Flower almanacs were popular in France by the early 1800s, providing facts and poems about flowers, and in 1819 Louise Cortambert (writing as Madame Charlotte de La Tour) published the first floriography dictionary, *Le Langage des fleurs* (*The Language of Flowers*). She claimed the language to be ancient and provided a series of meanings, some based on seasonal observations, others on medical properties and yet others on legends associated with the flowers.

Other dictionaries followed. Many of them, including my favourite Mrs Burke's *The Illustrated Language of Flowers* (1858), offered a list of flowers with their associated meanings first, followed by the meanings with their associated flowers. You could decode the flowers you received using the first half of the book, and decide what flowers to send using the second half.

Plenty of recent books also explain flower meanings, but you need to make sure the recipient of your gift is using the same source as you! For example, yellow roses in Burke's system often mean "a decrease of love", while in other dictionaries they indicate jealousy or adultery, and a lot of florists now claim they mean friendship! I'm not sure when yellow roses changed their meaning, but picking the wrong one could lead to some very awkward conversations.

So if I wanted to send a message of affection, mossy saxifrage (*Saxifraga bryoides*), pear (*Pyrus communis*) or sorrel (*Rumex acetosa*) would all do the trick. A four-leaf clover (*Trifolium*) meant "be mine". Syrian mallow (*Hibiscus syriacus*) meant you were "consumed

✳ by love", while red tulips (*Tulipa gesneriana*) meant a declaration of love.

If you were going away on holiday, you could send forget-me-nots (*Myosotis sylvatica*) to help keep you in your lover's mind. White roses (*Rosa*) meant "I am worthy of you" and red chrysanthemums (*Chrysanthemum × morifolium*) simply meant "I love". You could send compliments through buttercups (*Ranunculus*), which meant "you are radiant with charms", or peach (*Prunus persica*), which meant "your qualities, like your charms, are unequalled".

More generally, both myrtle (*Myrtus communis*) and rose represented love, and flowers in the *Ambrosia* family meant returned love. So a person might send their crush red tulips, and if they got *Ambrosia* in return? They're on to a winner!

'WHICH WILL YOU TRY?

Most of the practices in this chapter require plants you can easily source, and growing plants yourself is both thoroughly rewarding and a simple way to access the ingredients you need. Who knows, maybe all this focus on plants is a cunning ruse to get you to the garden centre, where you'll bump into a green-fingered future partner?

As an easy way to get started in using plants in love magic and divination, why not look up some of the Victorian floriography dictionaries? You can find many of them for free online in the Internet Archive. Practise composing symbolic messages by sending plants or photos of flowers to your friends while you work up the nerve to send flowers to your crush.

CHAPTER 5

OMENS
OF LOVE

The seeking of omens is an ancient form of divination that relied upon a person paying attention to signs in their environment. Some practices, such as augury, in which the will of the gods was divined from the appearance and flight pattern of birds, were done at specific times and required highly trained and experienced diviners who knew how to interpret what they saw (although I would be keen to know how many of them felt confident passing on bad news to their king).

Other omens required no training to interpret and were passed on through word of mouth. They might relate to something specific that you might not ordinarily encounter, making them easier to spot during the course of your day, and you would interpret them within a context that made sense to you. For example, seeing five women knitting together meant a wedding would happen.[155] If you were not of marriageable age, seeing five women knitting together would likely mean nothing. Yet if you were hoping to marry, or you knew someone in that situation, the knitting women suddenly became a positive omen.

Other omens would dictate your actions, in much the same way as people might change their behaviour according to a superstition. For example, it was a bad omen to start writing a love letter and not finish it on the same day. If you did this and sent the letter, the letter would either go astray or be received coldly, or the recipient would somehow be in trouble.[156]

Some of the omens below seem closer to superstitions, particularly those related to mundane actions such as stirring a fire with a poker, yet they still rely upon a person interpreting the action and its results. As we shall see in the hearth fire section, those interpretations varied depending on where they were recorded, which shows these omens were by no means universal and may perhaps have only been followed in the location where a folklorist preserved them in writing.

Omens also became associated with particular days, and we shall examine a system of love divination specific to Valentine's Day. Others are observed in the behaviour of animals or in the weather. While some forms of divination, such as cartomancy, are active, with the reader engaging with the divinatory tool to get their answer, spotting omens is often more passive, relying on a person being cognisant of the omen and aware enough to notice it when it happens. We can't know how often any of these were practiced, or in some cases even if they were practiced, but they can still contribute to our understanding of our forebears' preoccupation with finding love or managing a happy marriage.

BIRD OMENS

One strange form of love divination involves practicing ornithomancy, or divination using birds, on St Valentine's Day. Some think ornithomancy became linked with 14 February because of a belief that birds chose their mate for the year on that day. This belief probably came from Chaucer's poem "Parlement of Foules" (c. 1382), in which the personification of Nature holds a meeting during which the birds choose their partners. The poem is remarkable as the first Valentine's poem in English literature, but it's likely that Chaucer was writing about this "marriage of the birds" in a symbolic way, as there is no evidence that anyone in centuries gone by genuinely believed birds mated on a specific day of the year. After all, however divorced from the behaviour of wildlife, including birds, we are here in the 21st century, people in Chaucer's era lived in an agrarian society and would have been well-versed in knowledge of the natural world.

According to this tradition, the first bird a single woman sees on Valentine's Day will predict their future partner's career and in some cases their character too. Plenty of different lists appear online, often in seasonal articles by newspapers keen to capitalize on 14 February, and it's difficult to work out if they're authentic interpretations that anyone might actually have used. That said, many of the lists agree on the birds and the careers they represent, and in many cases the choice of bird seems to be rooted in established folklore.

Glossary of Bird Meanings

BIRD OF PREY: Someone who holds a position of power or is a leader of some kind. Often refers to politicians or businesspeople.

BLACKBIRD: A vicar or a priest. A kind person.

BLUEBIRD: Someone with a good sense of humour, perhaps a comedian.

CANADA GOOSE: Someone devoted to their family. A very caring person.

CANARY: Someone who heals others, such as a doctor.

CARDINAL: A romantic person.

CHICKADEE: An intelligent thinker, possibly a professor or philosopher.

CROSSBILL: Someone who argues for a living, like a lawyer. Not someone you want to "cross".

CROW: This means there will either be no relationship or that you should leave the one you're in. While this sounds harsh, remember you can try out the tradition again next year.

DOVE: A happy marriage.

DUCK: A homely but stable person.

FINCH: A very sociable person, such as a hair stylist or salesperson.

GOLDFINCH: A wealthy person.

GOOSE: Someone who works in communications.

GULL: Someone who often travels for work purposes.

HUMMINGBIRD: One who travels, perhaps a travel writer or a member of cabin crew.

KINGFISHER: Someone who has inherited wealth.

MAGPIE: An entrepreneur or opportunist.

NUTHATCH: A person of knowledge, such as a scientist or mathematician.

OWL: A researcher or someone who works in academia.

PEACOCK: Someone who takes pride in their appearance.

PHEASANT: Someone who is hard-working, tenacious and tries anything once.

PIGEON: Someone who is kind, loyal and peaceful. A lifelong, happy partnership. Someone who is a homebody.

ROBIN: A seafarer or a person in uniform.

SPARROW: A naturalist or someone who is at home in the country or in nature, such as a farmer, landscape gardener or tree surgeon.

STARLING: Someone who works in a big company but still manages to make themselves heard.

SWAN: A creative person, such as a musician, artist, dancer or actor. A life partner.

SWIFT: A sportsperson.

TURKEY: An environmentalist or naturalist.

WOODPECKER: You will have no relationship this year.

WREN: Someone who is not driven by seeking material possessions.

Your environment will dictate which birds you might see, so don't expect to see a pheasant in the middle of a city – although if you did, I would take that as a highly auspicious omen! Some birds are less likely to appear as they're nocturnal, and others might not even live in your country or, if they do, they might be migratory.

Here in the UK, I won't see a cardinal in February, while starlings don't arrive back in my part of the country until March. Still, because I like trying these practices, I followed the tradition on Valentine's Day in 2024 and the first bird I saw was a blackbird – I would certainly hope for a kind partner!

Unfortunately, I was still single by Valentine's Day in 2025, at which point I saw a robin, so I will let you know if I encounter a seafarer or a person in uniform. The latter is a good example of how we can adapt these traditions, as today a person in uniform is not necessarily in the military but could equally be a paramedic, a bus driver or a hospital orderly.

The folklore doesn't actually say if the sighting needs to be of a physical bird or an image of one, though I would imagine a physical bird would yield better results. Another Valentine's Day superstition, recorded in Derbyshire in 1872, directed women to look through their front door keyhole early on Valentine's Day morning. If they saw one object or person, they would remain single that year. If they saw two or more objects or people, they would find a partner. If they saw a cockerel and a hen, it meant they would marry by the end of the year.[157]

Of course, there were certain omens that mean you could use ornithomancy to divine your romantic future on other days, not just Valentine's Day. For example, if a woman entered a park at any time of year and immediately saw a peacock, she would marry a handsome man.[158] Seeing three magpies together suggested a wedding would take place.[159] This latter omen contradicts the famous magpie rhyme, which predicts "One for sorrow, two for joy, three for a girl, four for a boy". Three magpies may seem counterintuitive for a wedding, which traditionally involves two individuals, but perhaps the third magpie represents the clergyman who marries them.

CAT OMENS

Animal behaviour has provided the basis for various forms of divination or omen-spotting through the centuries. Some have long since fallen out of fashion, such as myomancy, which involved interpreting the activity of rodents. Others have become stripped down to simple omens, although there is not always an obvious connection between the action and the interpretation. For example, it was a good-luck omen for a cat to sneeze the day before a wedding.[160] The omen doesn't take into account how dusty a room was or if there was some other reason to prompt the cat to sneeze, but presumably the omen only held if the cat sneezed without being deliberately made to. You can't force an omen! It also doesn't explain why a cat's sneeze would bring good luck to a wedding, given the relative lack of cat-based superstitions around love and romance. Still, it's an easy one to pay attention to if there's a cat on the premises the day before your wedding!

Staying with the feline omens, if you have a pet cat and a rat crosses the room without the cat noticing, it meant you would soon get a visit from your lover.[161] The clandestine nature of this sign, with the cat not noticing the rat, suggests a secret tryst while your spouse was elsewhere. Of course, cats will often do things that defy interpretation, so it's perhaps best not to look to their behaviour for omens.

WEATHER OMENS

It's hardly surprising that the weather would offer love and partnership omens in Britain, given that discussing it is this country's national sport! Wanting good weather on important occasions is almost a given, hence the saying that "Happy the bride the sun shines on," and the suggestion that sunny weather at a wedding would mean a long and successful marriage for the couple.

Cavalier poet Robert Herrick first recorded this phrase in his 1648 poetry volume *Hesperides: or, The Works both Human and Divine of Robert Herrick Esq*. The original line, "Blest is the bride on whom the sun doth shine" comes from the poem "A Nuptiall Song, or Epithalamie, on Sir Clipseby Crew and His Lady".[162]

You may have heard the second half of this saying, "Happy the corpse the rain falls on," though this comes not from Herrick's original poem but from the 1607 play *The Puritan: or, The Widow of Watling Street*, in which the eponymous widow declares "if Blessed be the corpse the rain rains upon, he had it, pouring down?"[163] So now you know. The two lines have been brought together and now appear on the internet described as "a traditional saying".

Speaking of rain, rainbows also provided happy omens for those seeking love. If you saw a rainbow over your right shoulder, you would be married in the summer, while seeing a rainbow over your left shoulder meant a winter wedding.[164] And if the end of a rainbow seemed to land on someone's farm, it meant there would soon be a marriage in the farm owner's family![165]

There's a love divination you can do in wintry weather if you find ice on your windows. Knock the window with your hand and count how many pieces of ice fall off. That's how many lovers you will have. It doesn't specify if that's the number of lovers you'll have at the same time, or over the course of your life, so you can decide that before you start![166]

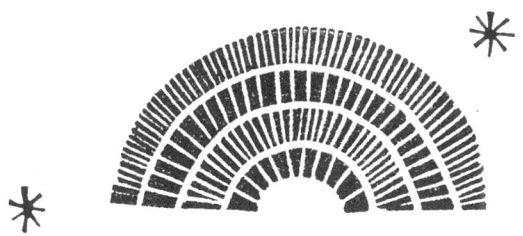

HEARTH FIRE OMENS

In Chapter 3 we explored the huge range of household items that people could use to make love magic or divine the state of their romantic future. Unsurprisingly, a home's fire could provide a number of different omens as to whether a person would marry and give an indication of the temperament of their partner.

If a woman stirred a fire and it then burned brightly, it meant her absent lover was happy and content.[167] Single women also stirred the coals with a poker and if doing so created a pure flame, this foretold a cheerful husband.[168] This is similar to the 1850s belief recorded in Lancashire that stirring the fire helped to test the mood of a lover: a blazing fire meant good humour, but a sputtering or inconsistent fire meant your lover had a similar temperament. In Pendle, Lancashire, if the fire burned brightly after you poked the coals, it meant your lover was on his way. By the 1890s, in Yorkshire, the omen had changed and the poking of the fire was used to check the mood of a lover at that moment in time, rather than in an overall sense.[169]

If you have an open fire and you're thinking of someone and the fire suddenly blazes up, then they're also thinking well of you.[170] Unmarried women could expect their sweetheart to call if sparks flew out of the fire, though that could potentially also indicate a visit from the fire brigade.[171] That said, according to a Suffolk belief, sparks flying out of the fire toward you meant someone disliked you, so it was important to note the direction of the sparks.[172] And if you could light a good fire using only one match, it meant you would make an amiable marriage partner.[173]

If a fire only burned on one side of the grate, it meant a wedding would happen soon, although an alternative version from Suffolk said a fire burning in such a fashion meant the man of the house was a bad husband. In Essex, a fire burning on one side foretold a death in the family, and in Worcestershire it foretold arguments in the house. All of which goes to show how omens can be interpreted in multiple different ways depending on where they are recorded.[174]

DREAM OMENS

Dreams provide an array of omens if you believe that common symbols mean the same thing to everyone who dreams of them. I'm inclined to think that dreams are personal to us as individuals, with the things that appear in them reflecting experiences, people and places known to the dreamer, but divination as a wider practice suggests otherwise! The dream omens explored here are distinct from the practices described in earlier chapters that sought to induce prophetic dreams.

While there are entire dictionaries devoted to dream meanings, I've focused in this book on three sources. The earliest of these is *Breslaw's Last Legacy: or, The Magical Companion*, published in 1784 and inspired by the work of conjurer Philip Breslaw. The book explains how to perform magic tricks and fortune telling using cards, revealing the secrets of legerdemain and other conjurer's tricks in the process. A section of the book focuses on the interpretation of dreams, noting that dreams in ancient times were the source of signs, warnings and divine information.[175] Unsurprisingly, many of these dream omens concern love.

The 1790s saw the publication of *The Universal Fortune Teller: or, Mrs Bridget's Golden Treasury Explained*, a book that purports to have been compiled by a woman who practiced fortune telling for 60 years. The title page also claims that the manuscript was discovered hidden in a rag in the thatch of her Norwood cottage. Though the overall veracity of the book is doubtful, it contains a useful section detailing what dreams meant in that era.

The dream meanings cover a range of outcomes, with a surprising number of the omens aimed at male readers, though this may be due to the prevailing literacy rates rather than men consulting fortune tellers more than women at that time. (Reading this book makes me think that Netflix needs a cute series about an 18th-century fortune teller turned matchmaker who contrives ever more elaborate schemes to introduce her clients to one another!)

My third source is a much later anthology from 1903, the *Encyclopaedia of Superstitions, Folklore and the Occult Sciences of the World*. This book specifies that you can only draw omens from dreams that occur naturally during ordinary sleep, and that you need to remember the dream clearly or vividly, discounting any vague or half-remembered dreams and any dreams that happen during restless sleep.[176] So you should certainly ignore fever dreams – when the imagery is likely to be at its most vivid and strange – as a source of any omens.

To all of the dream meanings offered below, we must add the belief that dreams that occurred on the 5th, 7th, 8th, 9th, 10th, 15th, 18th, 19th, 22nd, 27th and 30th of the month were held to predict the future, meaning dreams on those nights would come true.[177] By comparison, dreams on the 13th, 20th, 21st,

28th and 29th of the month would never come true. Or you could cheat and follow an Austrian custom that saw people leave mistletoe at the bedroom door to guarantee sweet dreams.[178] Others ensured they had happy dreams by burning hazelnuts and putting the ashes in envelopes that they popped under their pillow.[179]

Good Dream Omens

You might imagine that dreaming of roses, weddings or other positive imagery would be a good omen for success in love. For example, girls dreaming of young men putting gold rings on their fingers or tying on their garters meant they would marry.[180] The wedding theme of these images is clear. Likewise, dreaming of an unbroken chain meant marriage was in your future.[181] Yet according to the sources, a more unexpected selection of actions, images and behaviours also foretold good fortune in the romance department.

If a person dreamed that someone of the opposite gender gave them a glass of water, they would get an offer of an advantageous marriage.[182] It is unclear why a glass of water represented such a marriage, but it's a specific enough image that a dreamer would likely remember it upon waking. Meanwhile, young women who dreamed of walking in beautiful gardens could be sure they'd marry the man

they loved.[183] If another person was drawing in a dream, it foretold success in love for the dreamer.[184] Dreaming of fainting also foretold true love.[185]

Animals became important dream omens. Donkeys in dreams represented a range of things, including success in love.[186] Dreaming of riding a white horse that you owned meant you would be soon married to a beautiful or handsome partner; for women, it meant a rich husband.[187] If a pair of doves or pigeons came to your bedroom window in a dream, it meant marriage – and soon.[188] This dream omen is fascinating as it recalls doves representing a happy marriage, and pigeons representing a lifelong happy partnership, in the practice of ornithomancy.

Seeing your reflection in a dream meant you would find love.[189] Dreaming of eating ripe cherries was also a good omen as it meant you were in love and beloved by another.[190] Ploughs in dreams were a good omen for marriage, but it would take some time to happen.[191] If a man dreamed of seeing a pond, it meant a beautiful woman would love him.[192] A woman dreaming of a pond would accomplish her desires.[193]

If a man dreamed of a basin, it represented a female servant, and if he ate or drank out of the basin in the dream, it meant he loved the servant. If he saw his reflection in the basin, it meant he'd have children with the servant in question.[194]

Clearly, this dates to an era when harassing the staff was less frowned upon than it is now.

A man who dreamed of sitting on a woman's bed could take that as an omen he would marry the woman in question.[195] A dream of having a cook in his house was also a good omen if he wanted to marry.[196] That particular omen came from *The Universal Fortune Teller*, published in 1790. While it might suggest the outdated notion that a wife is simply there to provide domestic service, we could also be charitable and assume the man was planning to hire a cook, and the dream was a sign he would soon be in a position to welcome a wife into his household.

Other dream omens specifically foretold good news if you already had a partner. While dreaming of a ditch usually meant danger, if you were in love it meant you'd marry your current sweetheart.[197]

Surprisingly, even in the 1790 text, if a woman dreamed of having good sex with a man, it showed that she would soon be married to the man who courted her.[198] The omen doesn't specify if her sex dream should involve the man courting her and it also suggests the woman would have some knowledge or experience of sex in order to tell if it was good or not.

Dreaming of taking a warm bath meant you would marry your sweetheart soon, but the water temperature in your dream was important. Overly hot water meant arguments, and if the water wasn't warm enough, your marriage would be unhappy.[199] It's fascinating how often water turns up in dreams as a love or marriage omen.

Bad Dream Omens

While eating cherries was a good omen for love, other fruit were not. Dreaming of rotten fruit meant the target of your affections was false.[200] If you were in love and dreamed of bananas, it meant your sweetheart would deceive you.[201]

If a married woman dreamed of a cuckoo singing, it meant a man was going to try to seduce her away from her husband.[202] This likely refers to the behaviour of cuckoos in laying their eggs in another bird's nest, thus forcing the other bird to raise their chick as its own.

If you dreamed of sailing on a calm river, you'd find love, which sounds like a good omen, although if a man then dreamed he fell into a raging torrent, he'd fall for a married woman.[203] The symbolism in this dream omen is fairly obvious. While young women who dreamed of walking in beautiful gardens could expect success in love, if those gardens were carpeted in snow, the girl would be crossed in love.[204] If you dreamed you were drawing a self-portrait, it meant you'd receive a proposal you should refuse.[205]

A particularly icky omen dictated that dreaming of a pretty woman in a low-cut dress meant you would marry, but if the woman was plain or unattractive, you could only expect sorrow.[206] While the "pretty woman" part seems positive, the focus on plain women bringing sorrow shows how shallow humans can be, although I could argue that what is pretty to one person might be plain to another, so this dream omen is entirely subjective.

The loss or gain of body parts also acted as bad omens for those seeking love, and even those who had already found it. Seeing your hand with more fingers than usual meant a future marriage would fail.[207] We could probably read something into that about the extra fingers that often appear in AI-generated images! Meanwhile, if a man dreamed he'd lost his left eye, it meant he would lose his wife, while a woman dreaming she'd lost her right eye meant she would lose her husband.[208] It's unclear what it meant if a man dreamed he lost his right eye or if a woman dreamed she lost her *left* eye!

We looked earlier at weather omens that spoke of love, and weather appears within the realm of dream omens, too. A clear blue sky that became cloudy and windy in your dream meant you would enjoy happiness at the start of your marriage, but it would lead to poverty and arguments.[209] Seeing a rainbow in your dream meant your love would change – I'm assuming that's for the worse since I'm not sure how love could change for the better![210]

Dreaming of gold rings might be a
good omen for single women,
but if married women dreamed
of losing their wedding ring, it
meant they didn't love their husbands. If they later dreamed
they'd found the lost ring, it meant there was still hope for
the marriage.[211] In earlier times love possibly played less of a
factor in women's choice of marriage partner than financial
security, social status and family expectations. Finding the
lost ring again suggested that these women might have still
made a success of their marriage, even if love had not been
their main motivation in marrying.

Given the focus on interpreting dreams to find omens of
marriage, it's surprising to know that dreaming of marriage
was actually an omen of danger![212]

✦ RANDOM OMENS ✦

I wanted to end this section with three ways of reading omens that are not specifically related to love or partnership, but which you can tailor for that purpose. They're also incredibly easy to use, you don't need to plan for them, and their appearance is entirely random. *You* become the divinatory tool, because all three practices rely on your paying attention to the things you see or hear throughout an ordinary day – specifically chance occurrences that seem to answer a question. All you need to do for all three forms of divination is ask a question, either in your head or out loud, and be receptive to the answer. True, you might argue that asking a question makes the responses less like omens and more like divination, but you could also view the question as helping to hold your focus on whatever omen might appear.

Our first approach is transataumancy, or divination according to things accidentally seen or heard. You might ask yourself if you'll get a response from the person you matched with on Tinder but who has yet to reply to your opening message. You almost run into someone wearing an '80s-style "Frankie Say Relax" T-shirt on your way into work. The slogan catches your eye and reminds you of your question; the T-shirt is not a yes or a no, but rather a suggestion to stop worrying about it and try the "whatever happens, happens" approach. One word of caution: you can't manufacture bumping into your answer just to get the response you want to hear. Instead, you ask the question and remain open to the response. For it to be a true omen, you'll only recognize the answer when you encounter it.

The second, equally simple practice is cledonomancy, which comes from the ancient Greek idea of *kledons*. The Greeks (and the Mesopotamians before them) believed the gods passed on their messages through the speech of regular people via moments called *kledons*, which is when something you overhear answers your question. Maybe you're dating three different people and you're not quite sure which one to pursue things with in a more serious way. You mentally ask who you should choose, and then go about your day. On the way home from work, you pop into a supermarket, and someone walks past talking on the phone. They use the person's name in a positive greeting, and it's the name of one of your three choices. What you overhear clearly answers your question.

The final form of omen in this category is the random shout in a crowd, or clamancy. It works in much the same way as cledonomancy, with the shout that is distinguishable from the otherwise unintelligible noise of the crowd giving the answer to your question. Because cledonomancy relies on things overheard, it implies much closer physical proximity to the speaker, while clamancy can work well at crowded events or in busy places, such as markets, festivals or gigs. How much you want to base your romantic decision-making on any of these random omens is entirely up to you, but it can certainly be an interesting experiment to run. You might prefer to use it for lower-stakes questions, such as where to go on a night out or for a date, or you might be bold and use it for those issues you've been wrestling with for a while. Just remember, it's always your choice to follow an omen – or not!

WHICH WILL YOU WATCH OUT FOR?

Many of these omens remain applicable in the 21st century, such as the practice of ornithomancy or interpreting the behaviour of birds, although others might need to be adapted – for example, omens relating to hearth fires could utilize outdoor barbecues.

Deciding how you feel about omens depends on whether you believe that everything that happens in life relies on chance or is subtly guided and shaped by God, the universe or another such force. If you believe the former, you might read omens as random anomalies, but ones that still hold meaning through the available interpretations. If you believe the latter, you would read omens as messages from the force animating the cosmos.

Either way, you need no special tools to use omens, only an understanding of what the omens mean. With random omens, you could even dispense with the question and simply stay open to the possibility of something meaningful being seen, said or shouted in your vicinity. Ditch the ear buds and keep your ears peeled next time you venture into public, and who knows what snippets of conversation might contain a useful tip for you. Even if you choose not to act on any omens – and in some cases it might be best not to – simply being open to the possibility that the universe, or chance itself, might have something to tell you can allow a flicker of magic into your life.

CHAPTER 6

USING POPPETS

P oppets are a form of sympathetic magic, in which the poppet or doll becomes a stand-in for a person. Whatever is done to the poppet is then magically done to the person it represents. While the idea of such a ritual doll bristling with pins has become erroneously associated with Hoodoo or African Traditional Religions (ATR), mostly thanks to misconceptions in horror films and fiction about what the practices involve, poppets have been used since antiquity by cultures all over the world, with examples found in ancient Babylon, Egypt, Greece and Rome, and, closer in time, in English folk magic. Of course, such figures were not solely used in love magic, but rather for a whole range of reasons, both positive and nefarious. Egyptian hieratic papyri detail the making of wax figures that represented enemies of the pharaohs, hostile gods or demons, which were then burned to protect the pharaoh and the land of Egypt.[213] In ancient Greece and Rome, people made figures of lead, wax or clay to represent their enemies, which they bound and buried in an effort to keep such people at bay.[214]

One thing these cursing or binding poppets have in common with those used in love magic is that there is no attempt at realism in the casting of the figure's features. They were not intended to be recognizable as a specific individual; instead, the practitioner linked the figure with the person it represented through other means. Most often, they inscribed a name or included something personal such as some hair in the construction of the figure, or possibly simply named the figure as part of the ritual.[215] Some Roman and Greek figures were buried with rolled-up slips of lead inscribed with a curse aimed at the individual that the figure represented.

Ancient figurines may be made from clay, wood, lead, wax or bone, while later examples might be made of fabric, straw or even foodstuffs, as, yes, poppets can be edible! These ancient examples from archaeological sites were often made for specific rites, so were highly bespoke items, while contemporary practitioners might make their own poppets on an ad hoc basis, buy "blank" ready-made poppets that they customize according to their needs or even repurpose existing dolls for different uses.

Poppets became popular within contemporary magical practice because they work for a whole range of end goals, from hexing or binding people who have harmed others to sending healing to the sick or bestowing good wishes on a client or family member. As we can see from the examples found in Egypt, binding an effigy was thought to "bind" whoever it represented, although this could mean a range of things, including preventing a person from testifying against you, interacting with you or even

having sex with anyone that was not you. More positively, if you make a poppet of yourself and ply it with lovely things, compliments and positive thoughts, you might raise your self-esteem. In some schools of thought, if you make a poppet of yourself to attract love and "wake it up" (we'll cover that later), the poppet will continue to work its magic even while you are going about your day. It becomes a means of keeping the magic going without you needing to be physically present.

This chapter explores the use of poppets in folk magic. While they have been maligned by popular culture and can be used for malevolent ends, there are also many ways in which they can be used in love magic, and re-employed in the 21st century to help attract love in a more general sense.

IMAGES OF WAX & CLAY

We saw in Chapter 3 how Simaetha used a wax image to represent her missing lover Delphis, burning it as part of a rite to draw him back into her life. The spell she used was a complex one, involving burning plant matter, the spinning of an iynx wheel and the help of a goddess. What we're more interested in here is the wax figure itself. While the image represents Delphis, what Simaetha does to it does not cause him harm, as you might expect burning an image to do. Instead, she uses fire to fan the flames of desire in Delphis so he will return; what is done to the figure is also done to the person it represents. It is this use of a figure to stand for someone who is not present that leads us into our discussion of wax or clay images in love magic.

Another example of the use of image magic in Classical literature comes from Virgil's eighth *Eclogue*. The poem is in the form of a song contest between two shepherds, Damon and Alphesiboeus. The latter recalls various love spells in order to ridicule such practices, which suggests they must have been common enough for the shepherd to know about them (or, at least, for Virgil to assume a shepherd would know about them). Alphesiboeus's song is in the voice of a woman who repeats her desire to use magic to "draw Daphnis home" and comment that "[t]he traitor left me", so we might assume a similar motivation to Simaetha's, to draw back the lover who had abandoned her.[216] The woman makes two images for her love magic: one of clay and one of wax. She binds the wax image with red, white and black thread, and carries it around the altar three times before burning it in the fire.[217] The destruction of the wax image appears to work in the same way that Simaetha's spell works, although the derisory description suggests Virgil was less than impressed with people resorting to such practices. The poem could be taken as evidence that people did try such rituals to bring an errant lover back, but whether they were considered to work is lost to time.

Clay poppets in the historical record can be more sinister. In the collection of the Paris Louvre and available to view online is a clay figurine from Roman Egypt, dating to the 4th century BCE, which depicts a kneeling female with her hands behind her back and lead pins inserted into her face, between her breasts and legs, and into her hands and feet. It's likely she was used in a magical operation as she was found inside a terracotta pot with an inscribed lead tablet.[218] The Romans were fond of making lead curse tablets, but the insertion of pins into the specific parts of the body suggests a binding spell, perhaps against a former lover or to stop a current lover from straying.

We see magical operations in English folk magic in the early modern period aimed at making men impotent, and only able to sexually perform with the woman casting the spell, so it's not such a stretch to imagine a man performing magic on a woman to prevent her from sleeping with anyone else. It's worth noting that whenever or wherever these spells were cast, the magician was most often *not* her husband, and didn't want her to sleep with her spouse.

A magical handbook found in Egypt, dating to the 3rd or 4th century CE, included instructions for making a clay effigy very similar to this one, with directions as to where to insert the pins and what to recite while doing so. It seems the pins were intended to create pain in the woman's body to remind her of the man making the effigy.[219] Sometimes, the nefarious attitudes to women we see on social media don't seem so very new, after all!

One magical practitioner in Rome seems to have made poppets from a range of materials, including wax, which were then placed inside lead containers that have been found under Rome's Piazza Euclide. While it would be tempting to assume that these were intended as curses, it might be that these too were binding spells cast on behalf of the practitioner's clients to force targeted individuals to lust after them, as we saw with the Roman Egyptian example above. These clients were usually men, hoping to force women to desire them.[220] It's not clear if they wanted a long-term relationship with the objects of their interest, or if they just wanted to have sex with them.

In Egypt, a pair of wax figures moulded in an embrace and wrapped in papyrus were found buried in a clay pot. The papyrus featured incantations that directed a ghost to seize a woman named Euphemia, the target of Theon's lust, and torment her until she abandoned her family and willingly went to Theon. We can assume the figures represented Theon and Euphemia. While these figures were buried rather than burned, the effect was the same: forcing a person to submit to another person against their will, this time enlisting the help of a ghost to do so.[221]

Such practices were not confined to the ancient period. St Irene, a 9th-century nun, wrote about a novice attacked with such a spell. It seems an unexpected passion suddenly seized the girl, driving her mad with desire for a former suitor, and she screamed his name repeatedly while leaping around, seemingly possessed by an irrational need to see him. She even threatened to hang herself if no one brought him before her. St Irene and the other nuns prayed fervently for help, and two saints flew over the abbey grounds and dropped a package. Inside were two lead figures locked in an embrace; apparently this was the novice and her former suitor.[222] While it is unclear what happened to the figures, it is suggested the suitor was impressed by the intervention of the saints and converted to Christianity.

In later centuries, poppets appeared in binding rituals in English folk magic, and now their use was leading to accusations of witchcraft, including against members of the nobility. Think of Jacquetta, Duchess of Bedford, who in 1469 was accused of using image magic to compel Edward IV to marry her daughter (see page 8). Yet Jacquetta was not the first noblewoman to be accused of using so-called "image magic".

In the 1440s, Eleanor Cobham, Duchess of Gloucester, was accused of using poppets to murder King Henry VI. Her husband, Humphrey, Duke of Gloucester, was Henry's uncle and first in line for the throne as Henry had no children; clearly, if something happened to Henry, Humphrey would become king, making Eleanor queen. The accusation came after Eleanor engaged the services of Roger Bolingbroke, a magician and astrologer, and Margery Jourdemayne, a notorious cunning woman, most likely to use fertility magic, as Eleanor had yet to bear a child. While love magic was condemned for its interference in marriage, the attitude toward magical help with conception was more lenient. Nonetheless, in 1441 Eleanor was arrested, and the prosecution produced wax and lead figures made by Bolingbroke as evidence. These, the prosecution said, were to be used to kill the king, since melting, burying or otherwise destroying such figures could injure or kill whoever they represented (clearly, the methods and intentions were not the same as those used in the ancient period). Eleanor insisted that she had only wanted Bolingbroke to draw up a horoscope and that she hired Jourdemayne for help in conceiving a child.

Given the crude nature of the figures, there was no way to tell who they were supposed to represent, if anyone. Perhaps the wax figures stood for the king, or perhaps they were indeed to be used in a fertility spell,[223] to "draw" a baby toward Eleanor or to increase her fertility. The authorities erred on the side of caution and executed Bolingbroke and Jourdemayne before annulling Eleanor's marriage to Humphrey. She spent the rest of her life under house arrest, demonstrating just how dangerous practicing such magic could be. If the poppets were part of a fertility ritual, which seems most likely, then sadly they never got the chance to work.

FABRIC POPPETS

Fabric poppets are mentioned in accounts of the events in Salem, Massachusetts, in 1692–3, when between 144 and 185 people were accused of witchcraft.[224] Nineteen people lost their lives as a result. Various accusations focused on fabric or the clothing worn by the accused witches, with cloth poppets supposedly used to torment the victims.[225] Mary Lacey Sr explained that she could take a rag, roll it up and imagine it to be a specific individual, then whatever she did to the rag would be experienced by the individual.

Abigail Faulkner allegedly held a piece of cloth during her examination, and when she squeezed it, her apparent victim had a fit. Mary Toothaker's poppet of choice was a dishcloth.[226] Margaret Hawkes allegedly used two pieces of cloth, one of which had knots tied into it. Three of the apparent victims were terrified to see the cloths. Someone set one of them on fire, and all three victims claimed to feel a dreadful burning until the flames were extinguished.[227] How much of the "witches'" confessions was true, and how much of it was procured under duress, remains to be seen.

Witch trials may seem like a strange topic for a book about love magic, but once you see how poppets were used in the historical record, you can start to imagine different, often more positive uses for them. Fabric could be extremely expensive in earlier centuries, with access to textiles associated with a person's economic position. The link between a person's standing and the clothes they wore meant that fabric poppets held even more significance than images made of wax or clay. Poppets could always be made with offcuts or scraps and easily concealed about your person. Using your intended victim's clothing helped to associate the poppet with the person in a more tangible way than simply inscribing their name onto parchment.

So far, many of these ideas are transferable to love magic. In theory, a person might make a poppet of the object of their affection from a scrap of their clothes, and by treating it well draw that person toward themselves. Or they might make a poppet out of scraps of an errant lover's clothing, to draw them back into their life. As described below, a more ethical modern variant would be to make poppets to represent yourself and your unnamed love-to-be and bind them together to bring you closer. Or you could make a fabric poppet of yourself to attract love – or friends, money, good health or whatever you needed – into your life.

PAPER IMAGES

Some love spells were not designed simply to attract a partner or reveal the identity of a future husband, as those in the folk practices we've discussed in earlier chapters often do. Some spells found in grimoires could easily be described as domination magic, with the aim being to coerce a chosen individual into loving the person that cast the spell (or their client).

The Grimoire of Arthur Gauntlet includes one such spell that involves the crafting of what sound like paper poppets, although their intended use is far from benign or twee. While our focus in this book is folk magic, and grimoire magic represents a more academic tradition, it is worth examining this spell, as Gauntlet was a 17th-century cunning man who made his magic accessible to his clients in London. His spells often call upon Jesus, God, the Devil and a range of spirits, demonstrating the crossover potential of folk magic and Christianity.[228]

Gauntlet recorded the results of this spell as "experiments", including variations on the process. The spell would make sure the target could not sleep, rest, eat, drink or even stand still until they had done whatever was requested of them by the practitioner – this might be Gauntlet, if he used the spell for himself, or his client, if he performed the ritual on behalf of someone else. The ultimate aim was to cause the target to burn in torment from their love for the practitioner, whoever that was.[229] It is likely that it would be a man, given the use of "she" and "her" in the incantation, though the spell itself was called "To gain the love of Man or Woman".

The spell directed the practitioner to draw two figures on a piece of virgin parchment as big as their hand. One represented the practitioner, with their name inscribed on it with their own blood, while the other represented the object of their attentions. When the paper was folded in half, the images should lie on top of each other. The practitioner drew their own image on a Friday, and the second image the following Friday, with Friday of course being the day associated with Venus. Once this was done, the spell directed them to stand on the images three times a day, first under one foot and then the other, during the first hour after sunrise, at noon, and before sunset. In one of the experiments, Gauntlet noted putting the images inside a shoe. The grimoire provided an incantation to accompany the ritual of putting the images beneath the foot, which they had to perform three times a day for three days straight. It also directed the practitioner to send the target five pieces of gold before they finished the work, or within this three-day period. If done correctly, the target would love the practitioner for as long as he lived and the practitioner could set aside the paper.[230]

We can see from this spell that a distrust of poppets is not entirely misplaced. Here, the fact they are made from paper does not make them more innocent, or less dangerous, than their wax and clay counterparts. Certainly, a paper poppet would be far easier to use in terms of being able to secrete it about your person and carry it with you. That said, paper would be harder to come by for a less literate swathe of society. Also, the sending of five pieces of gold made a spell like this inaccessible for most people, so Gauntlet's clientele was likely the upper classes.

EDIBLE POPPETS

Our final class of poppet is the edible poppet, which offered a range of benefits, from the greater accessibility of ingredients to the easier disposal of the evidence! These edible options show that witches might not always use the traditional doll-shaped figures as poppets. In a witch trial in early modern Spain, a woman explained that a witch instructed her to put an orange in the hot embers of the fire and recite an incantation to make her intended lover's heart burn with love for her.

An alternative version saw eggs thrown into the fire for the same reason. The burning orange, or exploding eggs, stood in for the desired lover's heart.[231] This links to the use of wax effigies that were burned in the Greek examples we examined earlier. The advantage of this approach was its simplicity – no moulding of wax or clay required – and the ready availability of foodstuffs. While access to oranges in other countries would have depended on social class, eggs would have been easy to come by.

We've already seen nuts and seeds used in love divination practices in Chapters 3 and 4. Whichever food item was used, it needed only to be named to represent its target, although as I'm sure you've already guessed, if you want to try this, for ethical reasons I would suggest using "my future love", or something equally generic, instead of attempting to compel a specific person.

Yet when we think of edible poppets, we're probably more likely to think of something like a gingerbread man, or some other baked good shaped vaguely like a person. It must be said that not all humanoid baked goods are poppets. According to legend, Elizabeth I created the first gingerbread men, having the treat shaped and decorated to look like visiting dignitaries or prominent members of her court.[232] I say Elizabeth I created them, though we should probably credit her kitchen staff for the feat! Although these treats were not seen as poppets, a young woman might approach a cunning person to make a gingerbread man for her as a love token. Once it was prepared, she would just need to persuade her chosen young man to eat the gingerbread and, in theory, he would then fall in love with her.[233]

Tudor gingerbread was a very different prospect to the gingerbread we enjoy today, as it often never included actual ginger. A recipe from a mid-15th-century English cookbook instead requires honey, saffron, pepper, grated bread, cinnamon and cloves. The result would have been closer to a pudding, with a much more chewy consistency, although toward the end of the 16th century some cooks were using sugar rather than honey.[234]

Of course, edible poppets do raise a quandary when we consider their ancient use for binding or malevolent magic.

If we make a poppet to represent an individual with the belief that whatever we do to the poppet happens to the person, how do you go about eating one? Do you snap off the legs first, or the head? Or do we take our lead from the ancient Greek wax images, burned to recall a missing lover, with the destruction of the poppet being the part of the ritual that "activates" the spell? This is worth bearing in mind if you decide to make edible poppets in the form of figures. You can always inscribe a poppet of yourself with your own name using icing pens or add symbols that represent love or whatever else you're hoping to attract. Another benevolent way to use a poppet for love magic would be to imbue the gingerbread figure with the qualities you'd like to develop, and then consume it, thus transferring the qualities to yourself. Given this is a book focused on love magic, you might like to enchant a poppet to help boost your confidence, increase feelings of self-love or just to bring joy (who doesn't enjoy eating gingerbread men?).

USING A POPPET TODAY

Now we've covered the main types of poppets, how might you use them to bring love into your life?

One approach is to make a poppet to represent yourself, with the goal being to attract love into your life. But first you need to decide what material to use.

Wax and clay both offer advantages and disadvantages as poppet construction materials. Both are relatively easy to mould while soft, although wax can become brittle once it has cooled, and it can be difficult to handle when it is hot.

Clay traditionally needs to be fired to become "fixed", unless you work with air-dry clay, which, as the name suggests, hardens by itself on contact with air, or with polymer clay which needs to be baked. Clay offers the possibility to make more permanent poppets, which is why these types have survived in the historical record.

While melting a wax poppet would be easy enough, burning a clay one would be much harder. It could be smashed if destruction was important to the rite, but it is less obvious how smashing a poppet might be helpful in the realm of love magic. Making a figure to represent yourself and draw love your way is probably the easiest way to use clay in poppet love magic.

To make a fabric poppet (the most common form of poppet you might see in popular culture), cut two figure-shaped pieces from your chosen fabric – I've often found felt works well as it doesn't fray around the edges. Or you could use fabric from an item you've worn a lot (consider this an extreme form of upcycling). Next, sew the edges together, stuffing it as you go with scraps of fabric, proper doll stuffing or old bits of yarn, depending on what you have to hand. If you're making the poppet to represent yourself, then you'll need to add your name to it, along with a couple of hairs or nail clippings to "tie" the poppet to you. You might also add other ingredients you associate with love, either mixing these with your stuffing or making a sachet to go inside the poppet. The latter is helpful if any powders are included. Symbolic dried plants work well; rosemary, for example, was often used inside poppets to attract a lover.[235] If sewing isn't your thing, then you could create a basic poppet simply by tying a knot in a piece of fabric to represent the head.

If you make your poppet from paper, clay or wax, again add your name to it, and press the hairs into the wax or clay, or just tape the hairs to the back of the paper if that is your material.

A paper poppet can be made as fancy or as simple as you want; you could simply cut out a gingerbread-shaped figure or use

paper dolls with
interchangeable
clothes if you want
to be more creative.

Wrap threads representing colours
you associate with love, such as pink,
white and red, around the poppet. Consider
using three threads, perhaps in a braid, as the
number three often crops up in folklore and folk
magic. Depending on your material, you might
embroider, draw or inscribe a heart or a rose or
some other symbol that says "love" to you.

These decorative choices will all help cement the purpose
of the poppet in your mind, hence the focus on what *you*
associate with love.

When it's done, wake the poppet, perhaps by breathing on
it or giving it a kiss, name it (using your name) and tell the
poppet what you want it to do – in this case, bring love into
your life. Keep it somewhere safe and remember to "feed"
it regularly. Feeding isn't as strange as it sounds; you might

breathe on it to wake it back up, remind it of its task or anoint it with any essential oils that you feel are linked with love and romance. If you make a small fabric poppet, you can pin it to the inside of your clothes or carry it with you in a pocket or bag. Just make sure you don't lose it!

Another option is to make two poppets, one to represent yourself and the other to represent the type of partner you'd like to attract. This approach is a little bit more involved than the first one, but it also allows you to be more specific about what you're looking for in a person, rather than simply trying to attract romantic love as an abstract concept. Focus on the qualities you hope your future partner will have or the values they'll hold. Rather than inscribing their name, which you won't yet know, you can instead inscribe some of these qualities or values into the poppet. Position the poppets far apart once you've made them, and then the next day, move them slightly closer together. Repeat this for a week, bringing them closer together every day, and on the final day, bind the two poppets together with love-themed coloured thread or yarn. Paper poppets could just be clipped together. You have extra options if you use paper poppets with interchangeable outfits as you can choose clothes to suit the type of person you might hope to meet. However you do it, this method symbolically draws the poppets representing you and your hoped-for partner together using sympathetic magic. Store the connected poppets somewhere safe and carry on doing the things you normally do to meet new people, letting the magic do its work.

You can be imaginative about what you want your poppets to represent. We may think of them as human-shaped because that is what is found in the historical record, but the representational nature of the poppet is key here. You might shape a clay or wax poppet to represent a former relationship and then break or melt it, if you were hoping to heal and move on to a new relationship. Likewise, you could fashion two halves of a broken heart and fuse them together from soft wax to represent healing after heartbreak. You might make a figure to represent your ideal lover and burn it in order to draw them to you. Remember that burning the wax figure was not about destroying it but about inflaming whoever it represents with desire for you.[236]

If we use our imaginations a bit, we can even adapt the concept of the poppet show, as practiced by English children in the 19th and early 20th centuries, for use in love magic. Children used a shoebox, or a similar-sized box, to create the show, arranging the poppets with furniture from dolls' houses, flowers and so on.[237] They would charge viewers a penny, or sometimes a pin, to peek through a slit in the side of the box to see the scene:

"A pin to see the poppet show
All manners of colours oh!
See the ladies all below!"[238]

Boys made similar shows inside cereal boxes, using dolls and other items to recreate scenes from popular stories.[239] This might seem like a strange thing to include in this chapter, but I couldn't help thinking that if you are especially crafty, you might recreate a scene from a favourite romance novel or film with poppets that represents the kind of love you would like in your life. The poppet that isn't you will represent your ideal type of partner, rather than a specific character. You might choose to use paper cut-out dolls, fabric poppets or even tiny figures made from air-dry clay – you can always buy little model figures if you don't want to make them yourself. Making the scene acts as the spell, and viewing it every day could help to reinforce what you would like to bring into your life.

'WHICH WILL YOU TRY?

While much of the discussion in this chapter has leaned toward the nefarious, with poppets offering the opportunity to bind or curse people, hopefully you can also see the positive potential of poppets (try saying that quickly). I don't need to remind you of the overarching ethics of this book – don't use a poppet for something you wouldn't want someone to do to you. But whether you want to use them to attract love or a partner, or just to boost your own confidence, you have a range of options depending on your available materials and whether you want to be able to eat your end result. Given the use of ginger in love spells to spice up a romance, a gingerbread poppet does seem like a good choice! Poppets can be as basic as you like, or they can be opportunities to indulge your creative tendencies. As long as they contain a link to you (such as hair), and have been "woken up" and given something to do, then your imagination is your only real limit. Have fun!

CHAPTER 7

CARTOMANCY

People have practised the art of cartomancy – divination using cards – for centuries, though practitioners can still be subject to some highly problematic stereotypes, particularly around travelling fortune tellers. The cards themselves can be and often are misrepresented in popular culture, although, thankfully, the hackneyed plot twist that the appearance of the tarot Death card means literal death seems to be losing popularity at last! Interest in cartomancy has been booming for the past few years, with thousands of social media accounts dedicated to reviewing decks, suggesting spreads (card layouts) or exploring the meanings of different cards. Tarot teachers such as Meg Jones Wall, Chelsey Pippin Mizzi, Alice Sparkly Kat, Cassandra Snow and Lilith Dorsey offer different ways to read the cards beyond the meanings found in the booklet that accompanies most decks.

If the traditional card decks don't catch your eye, there are always hundreds of on-going campaigns to fund card decks of all types where you can find your favourite deities, pop culture characters or art style. If you are really adventurous, you can make your own card deck or repurpose card games for divination. Who knows what messages you might divine from Cards Against Humanity? A current favourite of mine is a card deck designed to help people learn the constellations, which I use for divinatory purposes, deriving meanings from the legends associated with the constellations!

Cartomancy doesn't only refer to tarot cards. It is also applied to divination using the much older playing cards, which likely originated in either southwest Asia or Tang Dynasty China. While it's difficult to definitively connect the playing cards used in medieval Europe with those used in either territory, they shared a lot of characteristics and people played very similar games with them.[240] The first deck for divination only appeared in London in 1685. In 1770, Jean Baptiste Alliette published *Etteilla: ou, Maniere de se Recreer avec un Jeu de Cardes* (*Etteilla: or, A Way to Entertain Yourself with a Deck of Cards*), explaining a system for using playing cards for divination purposes.

Yet another system of cartomancy is the Lenormand cards, named after Marie Anne Le Normand, who became famous for her deck of 36 divinatory cards during the Napoleonic era.

Oracle cards have existed in various forms since the 18th century, when they were referred to as fortune-telling cards. These early decks had illustrations representing a range of professions to tell interested seekers who they might marry or the type of life they might expect for themselves. They seem incredibly outdated now as most of the jobs listed are either no longer viable or have been made redundant by the advent of new technologies. Since the 1970s, oracle decks have taken a different form, themed around angels, deities, animals or plants, and used to provide guidance on a wide range of topics. Unlike tarot cards, whose meanings are largely fixed, contemporary oracle decks can have as many – or as few – cards as the deck designer wants. The cards can be read intuitively or using the guidebook that accompanies them.

This chapter focuses on the use of tarot and playing cards as a divinatory tool when seeking love or relationship advice. My focus is playing cards for two reasons. First, playing cards have always been a lot cheaper and more accessible than tarot cards – I bought my own pack of cards for the princely sum of £1 in a stationery shop! You no doubt already have a deck or two lying around the house. Given the emphasis in this book on folklore or magic practiced by ordinary people, it makes sense to use this easy-to-obtain item. Second, while a book like this can never hope to explain what *all* the 78 tarot cards mean, playing card meanings tend to be more straightforward.

I'll also provide a few simple spreads to help you determine what you seek in a partner, and how you may go about finding one, which you can use with playing cards, tarot decks or oracle cards if you prefer. The only cards we won't look at are Lenormand cards because they're a system unto themselves!

While I recognize that there isn't much folklore specifically about cartomancy related to love, we can apply other folklore involving cards to our purposes here. I have also included other suggestions from the world of contemporary divination. Folklore is a lived experience and we can always create our own traditions through the ways in which we interact with ordinary objects, such as a deck of cards.

PLAYING CARDS

The familiarity of playing cards means they are the ones least likely to raise eyebrows if you're using them in public – interested onlookers might assume you are simply playing a solitary card game they haven't seen before! If you are put off by the New Age associations of oracle cards, or the mystical reputation of tarot, playing cards offer a more grounded, less esoteric route into cartomancy.

Playing card decks contain 52 cards, divided into four suits of 13 cards. Some decks may have an additional joker card or two. The four suits are associated with meanings, while each individual card represents a different idea or outcome. Despite Alliette's attempt to create a definitive manual in 1770, there isn't a standard set of playing card meanings that everyone agrees upon, though there are some common associations. In some systems, hearts represent emotions or relationships, diamonds represent wealth, fortune or resources, clubs represent business or work, and spades represent conflict or problems.

As there is no singular set of interpretations, you can start with one person's meanings and then add your own as you get more familiar with the cards. Over time, you may alter your interpretations when you see how the cards show up in your life. Some writers suggest using spreads designed for

tarot or oracle cards, while others have created reading styles specific to playing cards. It's best to try a few approaches and see which works best for you.

Here is a list of meanings that I've collated from a few sources to get you started. You can see how few of the cards directly relate to love or romance, so if you want to use them for divination about your love life, interpreting them in a spread is going to be key.

Clubs

Ace: Solitude, self-reflection

2: Business partnership

3: Obstacles

4: Prepare for change

5: Good physical health

6: Fulfilling activities

7: Anxiety

8: Gatherings of people

9: Hope

10: A job well done

Jack: A friend or sibling

Queen: A wise woman

King: A judge

Hearts

Ace: A new romance

2: Sex or intimate connections

3: A wish coming true

4: Preparation for future excitement

5: Healthy relationships

6: Loyalty, long-term partnerships

7: Hatred

8: Flirting

9: Starting a new family/ home

10: Happy families

Jack: A baby or young boy

Queen: An amiable woman or a soulmate

King: A liberal man or a soulmate

Diamonds

Ace: A letter

2: Exchanging funds

3: Gifts

4: No news

5: Laughter

6: Good decisions

7: Lies

8: Gossip

9: Daydreams

10: Joy

Jack: Good news

Queen: A wedding

King: Wisdom with money

Spades

Ace: Sudden change/ endings

2: Fights or separation

3: Setbacks and hard challenges

4: Feeling "stuck" in situations

5: Illness

6: Bad decisions or temptation

7: Tears, of either sorrow or joy (depending on what cards surround it)

8: Arguments, poor communication

9: Grieving process

10: The worst is over, move on

Jack: A bad boy

Queen: A cruel woman, jealousy

King: A powerful man, anger

READING WITH PLAYING CARDS

A simple way to tell your future using playing cards is to formulate a yes/no question and shuffle the cards. Then go through them until you come to an ace. The Ace of Diamonds or Ace of Hearts means "yes". The Ace of Clubs or Ace of Spades means "no".

Alternatively, ask your question, shuffle the cards and draw a card. Red cards (hearts or diamonds) mean "yes", and black cards (clubs or spades) mean "no". Of course, you have a 50/50 chance of getting a red or a black card, so it is not the most nuanced way to use the cards.

One easy practice specifically related to your love life directs you to take the face cards (jack, queen, king) out of the deck and put them under your pillow on a Friday night, the day ruled by Venus. At sunrise on the next day, pull one of these cards at random. If you get a king, it means you'll marry soon. A queen means either celibacy or a delay in marrying. A jack refers to a cad who will be nothing but trouble[241] – and let's be honest, we've all met one of those. The suit gives further information. Diamonds mean a rich partner, spades mean a thrifty partner, hearts mean true love and clubs mean poverty.[242] If you drew the Queen of Spades, that would suggest you won't marry for a while, but your future partner will be thrifty.

Another simple practice involves the top and bottom cards in the deck. The top card provides information about external influences in your life; these are things that affect you but which you may or may not have any control over. They come from outside you. The bottom card provides information about internal influences; these are things related to your inner world, personality or desires. They come from inside you. Ask your question about your love life and shuffle your deck. Once you feel it is well shuffled, take the top and bottom cards and lay them side by side.

I just asked my deck about my chances for finding love in the first quarter of the year. For external influences, I drew the Ace of Clubs, which suggests solitude and self-reflection. I might take that to mean the chances aren't great, if solitude is an external circumstance! But for internal influences, I drew the Queen of Clubs, which suggests a wise woman. Perhaps I can use the period of self-reflection to become more wise. It might not help in the quest for love, but it gives me something to do in the meantime.

You can also use your playing cards in spreads designed for tarot or oracle cards. A popular option is to lay out three cards left to right, representing the past, present and future. I might ask a question like, "What do I need to know about my luck in love?" I've just pulled the 2 of Clubs, 5 of Spades and Jack of Hearts. So that suggests that, in the past, I've perhaps seen relationships as transactional (like a business partnership) rather than romantic. This has led to pain in the present, though the future could either hold a relationship or just a period of peace.

Next, if you want to know what to do with that information, you can use another spread. I've asked what I should do to prepare myself for love and drawn another three cards, this time representing the mind, body and spirit. I drew the 2 of Spades, 9 of Hearts and 4 of Diamonds. The 2 of Spades suggests a fight of some kind, though as this is related to the mind, it could be a good indication that some internal work is needed to battle unhelpful beliefs I might have about love and relationships. The 9 of Hearts would normally mean a new home or a new family, but in relation to the body, it might recommend changing my physical habits to create a "new me". That might look like managing my chronic illness in a new way, recovering from injuries or something similar. Meanwhile, the 4 of Diamonds for the spirit suggests a sense of waiting, or "no news", which also means there's nothing specific I need to do in a spiritual sense.

You can design any number of spreads to ask questions more suited to your situation. It's unlikely that asking the cards *where* or *when* you will meet a partner will yield much luck, which is a shame because, let's be honest, they'd be the most helpful questions to have answered!

PLAYING CARD SUPERSTITIONS

It's hardly surprising there was a range of love-related omens and superstitions attached to playing cards, given how common these cards were in everyday life. It's less obvious where some of these associations come from.

If you play cards, be wary about dropping any. If you dropped the 9 of Spades, it meant you'll quarrel with your partner.[243] Finding playing cards on the ground could offer a lucky or unlucky omen, depending on the card. If you were single, finding a Queen of Hearts face-down meant an unexpected obstacle would block your chances of marriage. A 9 of Hearts face-up was a good omen of joy and harmony, while face-down meant short-term quarrels. A face-up 8 of Hearts meant your children would be virtuous if you were married, or that you'd be successful in anything you did if you were unmarried. But face-down, it meant your spouse would cause you pain if you married.[244] A face-up Jack of Clubs meant you'd soon get a marriage proposal, while a face-down Jack of Clubs meant you would soon marry, though not the person you expected. The 9 of Diamonds brought bad luck whether it was face-up or down. If you were engaged, your partner would break things off, and if not, it foretold quarrels in the future.[245] A face-up 7 of Spades meant you would quarrel with your spouse or lover.[246]

TAROT CARDS

Tarot cards are sometimes presented as being somehow dangerous, scary and occult, but if you look at their history, it's likely that they grew out of something far less sinister – playing cards. A tarot deck contains 78 cards, with 22 cards in the Major Arcana and 56 cards in the Minor Arcana. The 22 picture cards of the Major Arcana may have originated in the portraits commissioned for the famous Visconti-Sforza tarot deck, which dates to mid-15th-century Milan and includes the cards you've probably seen in tarot artwork, such as The Sun, The Lovers, or Death. The Major Arcana begins with The Fool, which at card 0 is sometimes called the unnumbered card, and progresses to The World (numbered as card 21). Meanwhile, the four suits of the Minor Arcana likely came from playing cards, with the addition of the knight as a court card. In tarot the court cards are commonly referred to as the page, knight, queen and king, but sometimes the page becomes the princess and the knight becomes the prince. The hearts, clubs, spades and diamonds of playing cards became cups, wands, swords and coins (or pentacles) respectively.

There is evidence that people used tarot cards to play games, particularly *trionfi*, or "triumphs", in which the Major Arcana worked as trump cards. The decks only became known as tarocchi in the early 1500s, eventually turning into tarot. Occultists finally discovered the cards in the 1780s and began using them specifically for divination, although there is no way to know if early tarot deck owners used them for divination, just as we cannot know if people used playing cards for divination in the 14th century. The version of the Tarot de Marseilles deck in use today dates to 1709, while the most popular tarot deck, the Rider-Waite-Smith, was first published in the early 20th century. Many decks today are still based on the system, imagery and meanings created for the RWS deck. The esoteric reputation of tarot means that people will confidently tell you that it dates to ancient Egypt, though there is no evidence to link tarot with Egypt. Nor are the cards all that is left of the Library of Alexandria. It is also highly unlikely that they preserve hidden knowledge of 13th-century alchemists given they weren't invented until two centuries later.

Readers differ in their beliefs as to how the cards work, and this book is not the place to choose one approach over another. Some prefer to read the cards in a psychological fashion, with the imagery and symbols jogging loose different ideas and perspectives on a given subject. Others use the cards to divine the future, reading what is likely to happen by interpreting the images and following their intuition. And yet others still use the cards to connect with spirits, with the spirits sharing messages through the cards in a way the reader can understand. Famed cardslinger and Voodoo priestess Lilith Dorsey told me that any and all of these approaches can be true at once, since the "right" approach depends on the reader and why they're doing the reading. You might perform one reading for self-reflection purposes and another for your friend to help them process a difficult time. Lilith also told me that finding love is one of the top two subjects people ask tarot readers about, with the other being money.[247]

Tarot Cards Associated with Love

While some of the hearts suit in ordinary playing cards relate to love and relationships (see page 203), there are a few more cards with love associations to choose from in tarot. Indeed, the tarot cups suit often refers to emotions, although that isn't always specifically in relation to romance. Love exists in many forms, after all. But you're reading this book, so you're likely here for romantic love.

Of the Major Arcana, I'd argue the most obvious love-themed tarot card would be The Lovers, though with a caveat. Not all decks have The Lovers, instead featuring The Lover, which was a much earlier manifestation of the card. While some writers refer to The Lovers as a card representing a union of some kind, it can also indicate a choice you need to make rather than a relationship; in the Tarot de Marseille deck, for example, we see one figure having to choose between two lovers, illustrating the association with decision-making.

Some versions depict the lovers as Adam and Eve, raising ideas of temptation – which doesn't feel very romantic! Other cards in the Major Arcana could refer to love and relationships depending on the context, such as The Sun (representing success, joy and celebration) or The Empress (representing healthy boundaries, abundance, fertility and a nurturing presence).

If we turn to the Minor Arcana, the cups suit offers the most likely cards for love and romance. The Ace of Cups can represent the beginning of something, a cup overflowing with positive feelings and generally a good time to be had. The 2 of Cups is often described as the partnership card, often referring to a new or thriving relationship. I'd argue the 3 of Cups could also be useful as it often suggests joy or celebration through friendship, and falling in love with a friend doesn't sound like a bad situation! The 10 of Cups is often the "happy-ever-after" card, depicting a joyous couple in a beautiful home with winsome children, and while that might not be your idea of a "happy-ever-after", it essentially represents emotional fulfilment and contentment. The 10 of Coins/Pentacles is also a helpful card, representing a life of abundance and opportunity, with enough going spare to build a legacy for your family. Back in the cups, the Page of Cups represents someone who wears their heart on their sleeve and is open to learning about themselves and their feelings, while the Queen of Cups is a nourishing and intuitive figure who connects deeply to their own feelings and those of others. Of course, all the cards can tell you something useful, depending on where they show up in the spread.

Now let's look at some methods for using tarot to find a partner, dig into your feelings about relationships and figure out your current situation. I can't go through the meanings of all the cards here, but there are plenty of websites and books to help you learn to read tarot – the teachers I mentioned earlier are a great place to start. I don't subscribe to the idea of solely using intuition, at least not when you're first learning, because tarot has a well-established system of meanings and you might as well get to grips with it if you're going to use the cards for divination. That said, if you've been reading for a while, you likely have other interpretations that pop into your head as you look at the cards and it's best to pay attention to those.

Using Tarot Cards to Find Love

While I would dearly love to provide some folklore or folk practices involving tarot cards, the reality is that tarot decks were not as ubiquitous in earlier centuries as they are now. Where people may have used tarot, the folklorists who collected such practices either didn't think to ask about them or chose not to include them. We'll likely never know which it was. The 18th-century fortune-telling cards will have been far more prevalent than tarot among higher social classes, being much easier to use. So the recommendations in this section come from my own practices. They do involve a lot of introspection because, unfortunately, here in the 21st century, the search for love relies either on being intentional about what you hope to find or trusting to sheer luck.

An easy one to begin with involves using tarot to work out potential obstacles to finding a relationship. Shuffle your deck while thinking of the kind of partner you want, focusing on ideal qualities, traits or even interests. When you feel ready, stop shuffling and go through the deck, looking for the 2 of Cups. Take it out, along with the cards immediately beneath and above it in the deck ("beneath" is the card that precedes the 2 of Cups when looking through the pack face-up, and "above" is the one that follows it. If you are working through the pack face-down, then these cards would indeed be physically "beneath" and "above"). The card beneath the

2 of Cups represents a potential block to finding what you want. The card above the 2 of Cups gives advice as to how you can overcome or resolve that.

I always find it helpful to lay out the cards while I consider their advice. You might put them in a column, with the block at the bottom and the advice at the top, or you might put them in a row, with the block on the left and the advice on the right. It's important to turn the advice into an action step to give you something to do with the reading, otherwise you won't get as much out of doing it.

How might that work as an example? I've just drawn The Sun as the block, and The Chariot as the advice. The Sun often represents a sense of joy, celebration, optimism and delight, which seems like a weird card for a block! But it's possible that I'm more focused on the joy I'll feel at finding a partner than on the partner themselves, so my heart and mind are in the wrong place. After all, wanting a relationship purely for the joy of being in one isn't the best motivation.

The Chariot is more about determination, willpower and action, which is a helpful card to get in terms of advice. It's a reminder to focus on what I'm doing, so could encourage me to work out what sort of partner I really want, rather than just wanting the joy of finding anyone, and could also be a good kick in the pants to take the initiative in meeting new people. My action step might be thinking more about the partner I'd like, and then going to places where I'm more likely to meet someone with those qualities.

Another simple spread plays with the popular past–present–future format, with a slight twist. Instead of drawing a random card from the deck to represent the present, you can consciously choose one to symbolize how you feel about where you are now. Then shuffle, while asking about your romantic situation, and pull a card to represent the past, and another one for the future. Lay the past to the left of the card that represents your feelings about your current situation, and the future to the right.

As an example, I chose The Hermit, for its focus on solitude, introspection and searching for answers (well, it's a good card when you're doing research!). Then I shuffled and drew the 2 of Swords for my romantic past, and the Ace of Swords for my romantic future. There have been tough decisions in the past, decisions I didn't want to make, but my romantic future suggests ideas and inspiration being handed to me. The Ace of Swords is definitely a card of potential, so not the worst card to get! Both cards being swords suggests my romantic life involves a heavy degree of intellect and rational thought, which in itself could be a good nudge to lighten up and lean into feeling over thinking. You could also try this spread replacing the chosen card with The Lovers, or the 2 of Cups. If you are building a reading around a specific card like this, a good tip I once saw suggested by tarot scholar and reader Laetitia Barbier is to take that card from a different deck, which means you can pull it again for one of the other positions from your working deck.[248]

If you're trying to decide what you would like in a partner, you can ask the tarot that, too. Simply draw three cards, asking which qualities would be compatible with you. Think about what the cards you draw might represent. Even the so-called "negative" cards could be helpful here. The Tower becomes a person who doesn't accept the status quo and will tear something down that isn't working. The 3 of Swords might be someone who feels keenly, but recognizes that even negative emotions will pass. Any card that *really* doesn't sit well with you is also a good indication of what not to look for.

Finally, many readers suggest that you can use tarot cards beyond divination, often as visual aids to prime your subconscious to spot what you're looking for out in the real world. You could use cards that represent what you're looking for as the wallpaper on your phone, for example, or leave them propped up where you will see them around the house. If you keep meaningful cards visible, they can give you an extra boost as you try any of the practices in this book.

ORACLE CARDS

Oracle cards descend from the fortune-telling cards of earlier centuries, some of which may be found online. The Bibliothèque Nationale de France holds various French sets of cards in its collections, for example, or you can browse the Internet Archive to find decks such as the Teuila Fortune Cards. Isobel Strong, a diviner who used the Teuila cards in her own fortune-telling, provided images of the 35 cards in an article about them in the American periodical *The Puritan* in November 1899. The four cards referring to a dark-haired white man and woman and a fair-haired white man and woman are deeply unhelpful, their assumption that only white people might lie in your future revealing the drawbacks of using older decks in the 21st century. Strong's article was reprinted in 1906 in Britain, and the Teuila deck went on to influence Austin Osman Spare, the English occultist who created his own tarot cards in 1906. In the article, Strong explains how she'd originally acquired a set of cards in San Francisco and used them to read the fortunes of royalty while touring Hawaii. She predicted that Prince Oscar of Sweden would marry for love, and years later he did indeed abdicate to marry a woman he loved.[249] How wonderful for our purposes here that her first recollection of the cards involved reading a love fortune!

Oracle cards are much more fluid than tarot cards. While tarot decks always contain 78 cards, divided into the Major Arcana and the four suits of the Minor Arcana, oracle cards contain as many cards as their creator wants them to have. They come in a huge array of themes, from animals and plants to deities and other spiritual beings. Their meanings depend on the artwork and the messages chosen by their creator, though you can also read the cards according to your own intuition. Some oracle cards feature keywords, much like the 18th-century fortune-telling cards, while others require you to read lengthy explanations in the guidebook.

As with the tarot, some people read oracle cards as a vehicle for passing on messages, perhaps about the future, from gods, spirits or other higher beings. Others read them as a set of psychological prompts, giving you different perspectives on situations or events. You can use the same spreads for either approach, but you'll interpret the answers differently, mainly because it's hard to use the cards to predict the future if you're simultaneously employing them as a psychological tool.

As oracle decks are so different, it's more difficult to provide insights into the meaning of individual cards here. If you do want to experiment with different decks, then the retail platform or creator's website often allows you to choose a single card online, which can help you test the feel of a deck before you buy it.

You might wish to use oracle cards to explore a series of questions about how to find love or develop an existing relationship. To answer a question, shuffle the deck and lay out the cards in spreads. You can use one of the more complex spreads described online or in the deck guidebook, or choose from an array of simple three-card spreads, which are much easier and less daunting to work with. The three cards might refer to:

past / present / future

mind / body / spirit

you / the other person / the relationship as a whole

what you feel / what you think / what you could do

this month / this quarter / this year

or anything else you might like them to mean!

If you use spreads like these, you can see how the cards relate to each other, as well as reading them individually. What story do they tell across the spread? What does the positioning of the cards within the spread tell you? This can provide helpful information to guide your efforts to find, or maintain, a relationship.

WHICH WILL YOU TRY?

If you're new to card reading, oracle cards are probably more beginner-friendly than tarot, with the guidebook providing the information you need and hundreds of decks covering almost any theme you might think of. That said, if you already have a pack of playing cards in your house, then you have what you need to get started with cartomancy. True, there are fewer resources for learning to read playing cards, but you can start with one book (there are good options by Jonathan Dee and Cory Thomas Hutcheson) and work from there.

Perhaps I'm biased but I feel that developing a tarot practice is an especially rich, fascinating and rewarding way to gain insight into the options available to you when you're trying to find love, fan the flames of romance or build a lasting relationship. And whatever type of cartomancy you choose, there are many resources available online, as well as books and workshops to help you find your feet. Good luck!

CHAPTER 8

MAINTAINING YOUR RELATIONSHIP

Much of this book has focused on ways to attract love, dream of future partners or divine whether a romantic connection might ever be made. It's understandable that those without love would seek reassurance that it would be in their future, and for many in earlier centuries finding partnership was an economic necessity. As we have seen, a range of options was available to aid in getting a partner – ideally one of means. Given the tales of hopeful romantics duped by cunning folk who claimed to be able to produce a wealthy spouse before absconding with their fee, we can also see the need for folk practices that didn't require a third party's involvement.

Yet what happened once you *got* the partner? We looked at Aphrodite's magic girdle in Chapter 3, and there is some evidence that women wore similar devices in an effort to sweeten their new husbands after marriage.[250] There is also evidence in the historical record of magical services offered to improve the behaviour of an abusive or neglectful partner, which would have been helpful in an era when divorce was difficult to attain and came with a social stigma.

Other practices sought to ensure fidelity on the part of one or both partners or to bless a new marriage with health and happiness, which was no doubt welcome even for those marrying simply for economic stability. There were also magical means to bring back straying lovers, of benefit to those whose social standing would be affected by infidelity or for abandoned women left quite literally to hold the baby.

Where previous chapters focused on the *finding* of a relationship, this chapter will explore maintaining one. This includes the use of divination to ascertain the potential longevity of a relationship or someone's faithfulness, as well as magical practices to help encourage fidelity and improve an unpleasant partner's behaviour.

WILL IT LAST?

Perhaps the biggest question posed by those entering a relationship is "Will it last?" Given there are so many contributing factors to a relationship's success, it can be difficult to say, but folkloric practices exploring this question abound and aim to provide a definitive answer.

One approach takes us to the stunning Neolithic gallery grave of La Roche-aux-Fées in Brittany, France. According to one fable, the number of slabs that make up the dolmen varies, being 40, 41 or 42, depending on who's counting. If a couple wants to know if their relationship will last, they can find out by walking around the tomb in opposite directions, counting the stones. If they count the same number, the future looks bright.[251] By implication, counting different numbers suggests a rockier ride. Visiting La Roche-aux-Fées also offers a nice day out, so perhaps time spent together in historical locations is part of the recipe for success.

In Tuscany, lovers used a myrtle branch (*Myrtus communis*) to create a wedding contract. The couple broke the branch, and each partner took half before they parted. When they next met, they cried, *"Fuori il verde!"*, or "Out with your green branch!" The engagement was over if one of them couldn't produce their half of the branch. If both whipped out the twig, then it foretold a long and happy marriage.[252] I suspect this divination rested on the idea that only someone who cared about the future of the relationship would take care of their half of the branch.

If you had a partner who was dithering about being with you (I'm sure we've all had the "What are we?" conversation and it never gets any easier), then an onion could bring them round. You stuck the onion with new pins and roasted it, to "prick his heart".[253] In theory, this practice would prompt your partner to finally make a decision. While it's possible they could decide they didn't want to be with you, at least you would know this uncomfortable truth and could move on to someone more committed. This practice feels similar to the poppet rituals we examined in Chapter 6, with the onion standing in for the poppet that was burned or melted to stimulate the flames of desire in the loved one.

In Wales, people made blackthorn (*Prunus spinosa*) thorns into pins and threw them into wells. If they sank, their lover was insincere.[254] It's interesting that this practice does not appear to be gendered, leaving it available for any partner who was unsure of their other half's intentions. Blackthorn represented difficulty in the Victorian language of flowers, and perhaps this practice therefore relates to the difficulty of knowing what someone really feels about you.[255]

St John's wort (*Hypericum perforatum*), the sunny yellow flower that blooms in the northern hemisphere around the summer solstice, also appears in love divination. The red patches on the leaves would "bleed" if your intended loved you, however if the liquid released was colourless, the match was said to bedoomed.[256]

Meanwhile, in Brittany, young people went to a local standing stone or dolmen on St John's Eve to carry out a ritual to see if their lovers were faithful. Men wore bunches of green wheat while women wore flax blossoms. The hopeful attendees danced around the stone before laying their wreaths on it. If their wreath remained fresh over the next few days, they could trust their lover. If it shrivelled within a day or two, their love would not last.[257]

Paying attention to your dreams could also be instructive. If you dreamed of dandelions, it meant your loved one was lying to you.[258] It doesn't say what they were lying to you about, so it's unclear if this relates to fidelity or wider communication issues within the relationship. That said, it's likely that the lie was something worse than them fibbing because they're organizing a surprise birthday party for you.

CHOOSING THE RIGHT WEDDING DATE

Practices for ensuring wedded bliss often began before the big day itself. Choosing the right date could make all the difference to how well or how long the marriage lasted. Any date after 15 June was said to be propitious, although in fact the whole month was a good choice, as it was named for Juno, the Roman goddess of marriage.[259]

Fridays or Saturdays were considered the worst luck for weddings, which is strange given Friday's links with Venus, goddess of love.[260] Christmas Day was a popular choice, though that's because working people could guarantee they'd be off work. A short rhyme preserves the guidance for us:

> **"Monday for wealth,**
> **Tuesday for health,**
> **Wednesday the best day of all;**
> **Thursday for losses,**
> **Friday for crosses,**
> **And Saturday no luck at all."** [261]

There was also a prohibition on certain periods of the year, according to one particular saying:

"If you marry in Lent,
You will live to repent.
Marry in May,
Rue for aye." [262]

It is difficult to know whether this type of folklore was genuinely practiced or just vaguely repeated. Folklorist George Monger refers to these sorts of sayings and proverbs as "armchair folklore", drawn from a pool of untested information.[263] When it comes to superstitions about days on which to marry, we can test them against the evidence to see what people actually did.

Before 1968, it turns out, May was more popular for weddings than months such as February or November, meaning people may not have considered the month unlucky. In the 1950s and '60s, changes to tax allowances for married couples meant it was more advantageous to marry in March (before the end of the financial year)![264]

These days, the weather is far more of a contributing factor to wedding month choices, although a wedding photographer I know told me that more couples are choosing to hold a small weekday ceremony to save money, saving the reception for a weekend. Who knows how a change like that will appear in future folklore?

WEDDING OMENS – GOOD & BAD

People collected a range of wedding omens, believed to indicate whether the marriage was blessed or not. It was lucky to see a rainbow on your wedding day or to have the sun shine on your back.[265] Meanwhile, some thought you could drive away evil spirits by dancing at your wedding, a practice that continues at weddings around the world even now. The groom should carry the bride over the threshold to ensure she doesn't trip or fall, which was considered a bad omen (so carrying her was a way to avoid a bad omen rather than to specifically bring good luck).[266]

It's long been considered propitious for a chimney sweep to kiss the bride and shake hands with the groom.[267] Various sources offer reasons as to why this might be so; for example, folklorist Maria Leach highlights the magical properties associated with soot and ashes, especially around fertility, suggesting that the sweep might be somehow passing those positive properties onto the bride by giving her a quick peck.[268]

Naturally, weddings also attracted a series of bad omens. These included meeting a funeral on the way to the church, the church clock striking during the ceremony, or getting married during a thunderstorm.[269] In the Borders, it was considered unlucky if swine crossed a wedding party's path.[270] More widely in Scotland, it was considered bad luck to hold the wedding after sunset; if you did, the bride could only look forward to "a joyless life, the loss of children and an early grave".[271]

There was also a rhyme around name changing: "Change the name and not the letter, change for the worse and not the better" referred to the first letter of the surname.[272] So if you were Elizabeth Smith and you married Paul Stapleton, this was considered bad luck, while marrying Paul Anderson would be fine. It was also considered bad luck for anyone to use the bride's maiden name after the wedding or to use her married name beforehand, presumably because continuing to use her maiden name recalled her unmarried status, while using her married name too early risked tempting fate.[273]

Finally, it was a bad omen if the horses pulling the bridal carriage refused to move. This tradition now applies to a car that is unable to start instead, an example of lore changing to fit the times.[274]

BLESSING THE NEWLYWEDS

You may have seen the popular custom of tying old shoes to the car the newly married couple will use to leave their wedding venue. This derives from a much older practice in which old shoes were thrown after people setting off on a journey to wish them luck.[275] It appears in 1546 in *Proverbs* by John Heywood:

"For good lucke, cast an olde shoe after mee."[276]

The belief expanded so that throwing an old shoe brought luck to whatever endeavour the person was doing, including getting married. Queen Victoria even recorded the practice in her journal on 7 September 1855. When the royal party arrived at Balmoral, someone threw an old shoe after them into the house to bring good luck.[277] At least, that was the assumption as to why someone threw a shoe at the monarch!

Many of the superstitions about ensuring marital bliss are related to things the bride needed to do, rather than the groom. Perhaps the most famous is the "Something old" rhyme, which was first recorded in 1883:

"Something old, something new,
Something borrowed, something blue,
And a lucky sixpence in her shoe!"²⁷⁸

The "old" item brought good luck for your family, the "new" item brought new luck for yourself in the present, the "borrowed" item brought loyalty, the "blue" item brought fidelity, while the lucky sixpence brought wealth. Some believed that the borrowed item needed to have come from a former bride who wore it at her own wedding. Obviously, this only worked if her marriage had turned out well. New brides favoured the veil as being the luckiest item to borrow.²⁷⁹ After all, if you didn't need the veil after your own wedding, it implied you wouldn't need to marry again!

As for "something blue", wearing white at a wedding is a relatively new concept. It doesn't apply in all cultures, being considered inappropriate in India, for example, where it is associated with funerals, and wearing white is not even a time-honoured tradition in Britain. Queen Victoria only made it popular in 1840, with the white dress suddenly signifying purity. Before white dresses became commonplace, a rhyme existed to help you choose the colour:

"Married in green, ashamed to be seen,
Married in grey, will go far away,
Married in red, wish yourself dead,
Married in blue, always be true,
Married in yellow, ashamed of your fellow,
Married in black, wish yourself back,
Married in pink, of you he'll think,
Married in white, sure to go right."[280]

Blue was especially favoured, and the colour was often associated with true love and loyalty.[281] One of the reasons people feared being married in green was the belief that green was the fairies' colour, and they'd feel insulted if humans wore it, leading them to "destroy the wearer".[282] The bride shouldn't make her own dress, and ideally she would leave one design element off the dress until she left for church, such as a ribbon or bow. She would only add this at the last minute.[283] Once the dress was complete, the bride couldn't look at it in the mirror. And we all know the belief that the groom couldn't see the dress before the wedding.

I mentioned earlier the real reason for the bridegroom needing to carry the bride across the threshold. Yet in the

1850s, there was a belief in Yorkshire that when newlyweds first entered their new home, someone had to bring in a hen and prompt it to cackle. This would, apparently, attract good luck. A Scottish variation from the 1870s suggested that a bride hearing a hen cackle as she crossed the threshold would mean she'd be a happy mother and a contented wife. In Somerset in the 1920s, a bride that heard hens cackle on the eve of her wedding would be a happy mother and enjoy her life.[284] These threshold superstitions have fallen out of favour, including one Edinburgh tradition recorded in 1818 that recommended the bride be greeted at the door of her new home by an existing female member of the household, led to the fireplace and handed the tongs, as their new mistress.[285]

Newlyweds were also advised to plant a cabbage (*Brassica oleracea*) in their garden as soon as possible to bring good luck to both their marriage and garden.[286] Similar customs were associated with other plants. During the Middle Ages, a new couple would plant rosemary (*Rosmarinus officinalis*) in the garden. If it failed to thrive, it suggested the marriage would fail.[287] Pine had links with fertility, and couples in the Tyrol region planted a pine tree when they married as late as 1950. In Germany, newlyweds planted a fir by the door of the house where they married.[288] People once believed that you could assure seven years of true love by using yarrow

(*Achillea millefolium*) in your wedding decorations and then hanging it over your marriage bed.[289]

Quince (*Cydonia oblonga*) also became associated with happiness at weddings. In 1725, it was noted in one household memorandum book that the groom's grandfather gave the bride a basket of quinces when she arrived at the wedding dinner to bring good luck. A married couple could cement their happiness by eating quinces together.[290] Quince has somewhat fallen out of fashion, perhaps due to its tart flavour profile, yet its association with weddings is a very old one. The ancient Greeks would throw quinces at the wedding chariot, which could be viewed as a fertility rite. Quinces, like apples and pomegranates, are filled with small seeds, suggesting a bountiful harvest to come.[291] According to the Greek philosopher Plutarch, a law even specified that an heiress had to eat a quince before being locked in the bridal chamber with her groom on her wedding day.[292] Classical historian Christopher A. Faraone suggests the gift of a quince from a groom to an heiress bride was intended to win her favour, since heiresses were forced to choose a husband from among their relatives to keep the fortune in the family. While the quince represented her hoped-for fertility with its many seeds, it might also act as a peace offering to a woman who didn't get to choose her own husband.[293]

You could also gift two early purple orchid (*Orchis mascula*) roots to a newly married couple to bring them happiness in the future.[294] If you are looking for something that's easier to come by, it was tradition to give brides hazelnuts (*Corylus avellana*) to pass on wisdom, fertility and good fortune.[295] In Devon, this job fell to an old woman who waited outside the church to greet the bride with a basket of hazelnuts. This isn't so surprising when you learn hazelnuts were linked with love, fertility, birth, knowledge and poetry.[296] The Romans even burned hazel torches on the wedding night to bring happiness to the new couple.[297]

Newlyweds stuffed lavender (*Lavandula officinalis*) into their mattresses to help encourage marital bliss, though I can't help thinking that would work in a roundabout fashion as lavender also traditionally helps to improve sleep, and well-rested people are more likely to get on with each other! People also give lavender sprigs to newlyweds to bring them luck.[298] This could have two reasons: having lavender in the home was believed to induce peace and the plant's scent was also thought to attract love.

Growing periwinkles outside your home encouraged harmony inside. In the language of flowers, blue periwinkles represented early friendship, while white periwinkles meant the pleasures of memory, so they made a good symbolic choice for domestic harmony. People also stuffed periwinkle leaves into the marital bed to promote fidelity and happiness.[299]

THE BRIDAL BOUQUET

Plants and weddings have a long association, with brides traditionally wearing floral crowns or carrying bouquets, and grooms wearing flowers in their buttonholes. In ancient Greece and Rome, bridal couples apparently wore crowns of sweet marjoram (*Origanum majorana*) to represent honour, happiness and love.[300]

The flowers chosen for the bridal bouquet could contribute to the success of the marriage. Myrtle (*Myrtus communis*) became a regular fixture in royal bridal bouquets after a sprig from Queen Victoria's bouquet was planted, supplying myrtle cuttings to bless future royal couples with the same marital happiness as she enjoyed with Prince Albert. Carrying myrtle is believed to preserve love, and growing myrtle on either side of the house promotes domestic peace and love.[301] Incidentally, if you grew myrtle in a windowbox and it bloomed in huge amounts, it prophesied a wedding soon.[302]

Victorian brides often carried fresh orange blossoms (*Citrus* x *sinensis*) to bring happiness, and some wore wreaths made of the flowers.[303] Putting waxflower (*Chamelaucium*) in a bouquet would also bestow happiness in marriage.[304] Rosemary was another common plant in wedding bouquets because its link with remembrance was believed to help the couple remember their wedding vows.[305]

A bride might pick a sprig of vervain (*Verbena*) and add it to her wedding bouquet to make sure her husband didn't stray.[306] In the Victorian language of flowers, vervain meant enchantment, so perhaps brides included it in their bouquet to "enchant" their husbands.[307] People also scattered marigolds on the floor at weddings because the flower represents constancy in love, and brides might include it in their bouquet for the same reason.[308]

In the West Country, bridesmaids carried sneezewort (*Achillea ptarmica*) in their bouquets to promote matrimonial happiness. The wedding feast included leaves of yarrow (*Achillea millefolium*),, also known as seven years' love, to ensure the marriage lasted.[309]

✦ KEEPING YOUR
PARTNER FAITHFUL ✦

While the practices I've described so far were intended to bless a new marriage and bestow luck and fertility on the happy couple, the remainder of this chapter deals with the harder side of relationships: remaining faithful (if you've chosen monogamy), drawing back a lover who has left or is romancing another, or improving the bad (and sometimes violent) behaviour of a partner. Of course, today the advice for anyone experiencing physical or emotional abuse is not to try to improve their partner's behaviour but to seek support in leaving their abuser.

Let's look at those charms used to promote fidelity first. If you wanted to keep your lover faithful, you had to steal a mistletoe (*Viscum album*) berry and swallow it. Mistletoe berries are poisonous though, so do not try this one. Next, you used a pin to prick your lover's initials onto a mistletoe leaf, and then stitch it into your clothes over your heart. They would remain attached for as long as the leaf remained in place.[310]

In Sweden, people sewed garlic (*Allium sativum*) and thyme (*Thymus*) into the bridegroom's clothes to prevent him from being bewitched on his way to the church.[311] A woman might hide caraway (*Carum carvi*) seeds in her husband's pockets to keep him from being lured away by other women.[312]

As early as the Middle Ages, caraway was a common component in love potions to stop lovers from straying.[313] Alternatively, a woman might wear a sprig of skullcap (*Scutellaria*) to stop her husband from falling for the charms of another.[314] A girl might hide a four-leaf clover (*Trifolium*) in her partner's shoe to keep him from straying, especially if he was off travelling.[315]

In Germany, people wore parsley (*Petroselinum crispum*) to keep their partner faithful. The dried form of the plant was a popular ingredient in any spells you worked for your relationship. There was also a simple parsley charm you could make to ensure your partner didn't stray. Draw your initials entwined with theirs on a small piece of paper. Put the paper with a pinch of parsley in a pouch and hide the pouch in your partner's coat pocket or bag.[316]

Young Greeks used poppies (*Papaver*) to check if their lover remained loyal to them. They would put a petal in their left palm and hit it with their right hand. A broken petal meant their lover was true. An unbroken petal implied their lover was unfaithful, which sounds counterintuitive as you might expect the opposite to be the case. This practice passed into Rome and made its way into 19th-century Italian folk practices.[317]

These options involve one partner distrusting the other – or, at least, fearing the possibility of their partner being tempted. Not all the fidelity charms featured a degree of subterfuge. Some were even actively embraced by the couple, offering an interesting opportunity to deepen a romantic bond. Newlyweds might rub the same basil (*Ocimum basilicum*) leaf over their hearts in a joint display to help with fidelity. In Italy, basil was used as a love token, so this belief may have originated there.[318]

Finally, there were other measures that sought to avoid driving away a partner. For example, people took care not to turn any burning lumps of peat in the fire if their daughter's lover was in the house. If they did, he would not return.[319]

IMPROVING A PARTNER'S BEHAVIOUR

While unhappy husbands could simply leave the household, the same option was largely unavailable to unhappy wives, who were restricted by social conventions and poor access to funds. Without the option to leave, an unhappy wife might instead turn to magic to help soothe an angry husband's temperament or encourage him to behave more kindly toward her. In the 1470s, Joan Squyer started washing her husband's shirts in holy water, which apparently tamed his behaviour.[320] Girls hid sprigs of lavender under the pillows of their beloved to help them think loving thoughts.[321] This suggests either an attempt to cajole a disinterested lover to commit or a desperate way to persuade a bad-tempered partner to behave better.

Unless a wife knew any similar folkloric remedies to sweeten poor behaviour, she would likely seek the help of the cunning folk. Different magical practitioners offered different approaches, depending on their experience. Written charms appear in the historical record, often crafted to coincide with favourable astrological events. In the 1590s in Canterbury, for example, a woman named Alice Suttill sought the help of cunning man Thomas Fansome in making her husband love her. It seems Fansome was originally unwilling to help, but Alice was persistent enough that he provided her with a paper charm to wear around her neck. While it is unclear what was written on the paper, Fansome described it as being a collection of prayers.[322] It seems Alice never took it off, which suggests how desperate she was for her husband to love her. I can't help feeling rather sorry for her.

Unfortunately, a charge was levied at Alice and Fansome of using magic to kill William, rather than improve his behaviour. Was the charm actually intended to murder William and thus solve Alice's problem? Or did William feel so guilty and defensive about his behaviour driving Alice to magic that he decided to accuse her of being a witch? It is also possible that an unhappy husband might resort to witchcraft accusations to rid himself of his wife.

In 1559, George Throgmorton accused his wife Frances of trying to poison him, which is quite the accusation given his violence toward her if we are to believe her mother's claims about his behaviour. According to her, George not only beat Frances, but also bullied witnesses in the case. Frances defended herself by saying that she only hired magical practitioners for their help in improving her husband's behaviour. Given the relative social standing of each partner, with Frances the daughter of a baron and George part of the gentry, it seems unlikely that she would try to murder him for financial gain.[323] It also demonstrates the danger of seeking magical help in taming a vicious partner, since consulting a cunning person could lead to accusations of attempted murder.

Meanwhile, cunning man Peter Banks did a lot of business in 17th-century Newcastle upon Tyne, selling all sorts of magical contracts. Not all of them were for love; he also sold licences to sailors that he claimed would prevent them drowning at sea. They only lasted a year, so the sailors had to return to renew them. Confirmation bias no doubt told them that if they survived long enough to renew the licence, then it must have worked! But for our purposes, he also sold written charms to make a husband be nice to his wife. As with the sailors' licences, they were set to expire after a period of time, so if a charm worked, the wife had to renew the magic. It seems like a shrewd business move, and a precursor to the subscription model we're all familiar with now.

One woman, Jane Crossby, paid Banks two shirts and 10 shillings for a year-long contract. Apparently, her husband's behaviour changed for the better, though for some reason Jane decided not to renew, and her husband returned to his bad-tempered self.[324] We will never know if Banks' charm was the reason for the change of behaviour or whether this was all entirely coincidental, and the records don't reveal if Jane decided to take out another lease at a later date!

BRING BACK A STRAYING LOVER

The other area in which cunning folk offered their services around maintaining relationships, rather than simply attracting love, was to bring back an unfaithful or straying lover, whether this was an unwed sweetheart or a spouse. When a woman in Oldham named Sarah Ann Tomlinson went to visit a fortune teller, it was revealed that her husband had been unfaithful for over six years. Sarah Ann wanted to leave him, but the fortune teller warned her that her faithless husband would sell her furniture. Whether this was true or not is by the by, as the fortune teller sold her a written charm for 7 shillings that was designed to improve her husband's behaviour if she wore it over her heart.[325] The fortune teller also advised her on which herbs to add to his tea, which parts of the Bible to read, and how to burn his urine as she recited the Lord's Prayer. Sadly, we have no record as to whether the charm returned her faithless husband or not, but the use of the Bible shows the important role Christianity played within folk magic.

People might also take matters into their own hands and turn to more accessible practices in an effort to save a failing relationship. Marshmallow (*Althaea officinalis*) could apparently draw back a straying lover if kept in a vase on a windowsill.[326] If a vase of marshmallow suddenly appeared on your windowsill, it clearly also had the potential to alert others to your knowledge of the infidelity and perhaps this alone was enough to prompt an unfaithful partner to curtail their activities (or choose to end the relationship in favour of their lover). In a much more subtle practice, keeping a common daisy (*Bellis perennis*) root under your pillow could also draw back your lost lover.[327] Of course, the big question in this area is, do you really *want* them to come back?

In the case of unmarried pregnant women, bringing back a lover who had absconded would hopefully force him to marry her. Cunning woman Mary Bateman offered a service for a guinea to make a man marry the woman he'd gotten pregnant. When this failed, Bateman tried to convince the despondent woman that her unborn child was blocking the return of her lover, and plied her with herbs to end the pregnancy. While this attempt was successful in ending the pregnancy, it unfortunately ruined the woman's health, and it is unclear if the man ever returned.[328] Infamous cunning woman Maria Giles charged a woman a dress and 12 pence to drag back her absent husband. When Giles failed to produce the missing husband, the abandoned wife went in search of him herself, tracking him down to Winchester two months later.[329] Clearly, she could have found her husband without paying Giles a penny!

WHICH WILL YOU TRY?

The wedding superstitions in this chapter are perhaps the best known, as many of them have been passed on from one generation to another. They are quick and easy to perform, and cost little or nothing, so there is no harm in adding them to the to-do list for the big day. You know, just in case.

We find the practices designed to check if a relationship will last being passed on in their simplest form through the "he loves me/he loves me not" games. Anyone who's ever been keen on someone will know the gut-wrenching anxiety of trying to figure out if their new sweetheart is interested or not!

Having an open and honest conversation will always yield better results than trying these rituals. Yet the prevalence of practices designed to promote fidelity, bring back straying partners or improve a bad-tempered or disinterested partner's behaviour are a cold reminder that love and romance have always been a difficult part of life for some. While fairy tales might have tried to sell us the "happy-every-after", the magical practitioners offering their services to mend a harsh relationship or sweeten a volatile partner's temper sadly demonstrate that not everyone will be swept off their feet by Prince Charming or while away their days with their dream princess. Thankfully, there are now plenty of sources of help available if you need assistance when a relationship turns out to be less than you'd hoped for.

CONCLUSION

This book grew out of a fascination I developed for love magic and divination while researching content for my Fabulous Folklore podcast. Over the months, it became apparent that I needed to look further into these practices. Now I've done so, I think the big lesson I've taken away from it all is that, yes, dating is incredibly difficult, lonely, disappointing and soulless here in the 21st century ... but the task of finding love has always been like that. We've just brought technology into the equation. And, surprisingly, while it would be easy for this realization of our enduring difficulty in love to make me lose hope that I'll ever manage to find a romantic partner, it has made me realize how fundamentally human it all is.

While we look at some dating behaviour as dangerous now, which it very clearly is, this book also shows how people were trying to force their will on others as far back as the ancient world. The more things change, the more they stay the same.

Clearly there is a marked difference between making a clay figure of someone to bind them so they can't have sex with their own spouse, and throwing your shoe at a willow tree to see if you'll find love that year. I decided to include malicious as well as harmless attempts at love magic in the book, because to ignore one and focus only on the other would result in a toxic positivity that doesn't acknowledge the ways in which we have attempted to love and harm each other for centuries, all in pursuit of human connection.

But let's focus for now on the central desire behind love. In the past, people might have needed to find a partner, to continue their family line, have successors in the family business or provide financial security in times when there were fewer earning opportunities for women. Despite this need, often driven by material considerations, there seems to have been a sense that people wanted to find love. While we can't ignore the dubious magical workings of the ancient world or grimoire tradition in which magicians aimed to force particular women to desire them or their clients, plenty of other practices see men and women hoping to conjure a vision of their future love or make themselves more attractive to romantic partners. The historical record is littered with examples of unhappy marriages, made mostly for financial gain or social standing, so it gives me some hope that despite this, people still believed they could bring love into their lives somehow. I really hope that the women who sought magical help to improve the abusive behaviour of their husbands somehow found peace and contentment.

This desire to find love helps to explain the focus in folklore on practices designed to see your future marriage partner, whether as a waking vision or in a prophetic dream. There is often a sense of excitement in descriptions of the practices, as people tried them out, clearly hoping to see whoever they had a crush on at the time. Divination was perhaps more accessible to most people than magic, and indeed people may not even have realized that they were taking part in such an ancient and time-honoured tradition as love divination. They just wanted to know whether they'd find love or whether the person they were with was being honest with them. Whether or not you believe these practices work, or just see them as a bit of fun that you can share with friends, giving them a go can help us to feel more connected to all the people who practiced them before us. And what is love, if not human connection? If you try any divination from this book and nothing happens, don't worry. Just assume that it didn't work because you haven't met the right person yet.

Folklore is a living, breathing experience that we interact with every day in our own cultural setting. By following folk practices, updating them and adapting them to suit our 21st-century context, you're slotting into that lineage of people taking matters into their own hands when it comes to that most human of all desires – finding and keeping love.

Feel free to mix and match the practices! Why not use playing card divination to check which type of magic to try? Or you might stick to seasonal rituals because they're well documented and you have multiple points throughout the year to try them out. Remember the 17th-century cunning man Arthur Gauntlet. He recorded his experiments in his grimoire trying out variations of practices as he sought to refine his process. I only ask that you leave the domination magic and the temptation to compel another person in the past, where such abhorrent practices should stay. Navigating the world of human relationships is complicated enough as it is without trying to make it even more difficult!

While it's rarely specified in the folklore, modern witchcraft practice would advise you to back up any love magic work or divination with practical actions. Go on the dates, speak to new people, be confident in yourself and above all keep persevering!

Who knows, maybe there are two people reading this book who each make a poppet to attract a loving partner ... and they end up attracting each other. If that happens, I want an invite to the wedding!

Even if you only ever take part in these traditions by texting photos of plants to your friends to send messages in the language of flowers, you'll still be adding a splash of love to the world, and Venus knows, we need that too. So have fun, stay safe, and remember to be excellent to each other ...

Bibliography

American Folklore Society (1892), "Marriage Superstitions in Scotland", *The Journal of American Folklore*, 5:18, pp.238–9.

American Folklore Society (1895), "The Origin of Playing Cards", *The Journal of American Folklore,* 8:30, pp.250–1.

Anonymous (1911 [1607]), *The Puritan: or, The Widow of Watling Street*, London: The Tudor Facsimile Texts.

Atsma, Aaron J. (2000–17), "lynx", *Theoi Project*, www.theoi.com/ Nymphe/Nymphelynx.html. Accessed on 30 September 2024.

Bailliot, Magali (2015), "Roman Magic Figurines from the Western Provinces of the Roman Empire: An Archaeological Survey", *Britannia*, 46, pp.93–110.

Baker, Margaret (2011 [1969]), *Discovering the Folklore of Plants,* third edition, Boxley, Oxford: Shire Classics.

Barbier, Laetitia (2023), "Dissecting the Tarot II: The Celtic Cross Spread with Morbid Anatomy's Laetitia Barbier" [Online Class], *Morbid Anatomy*. 9 September.

Bartlett, Sarah (2019), *Knot Magic: A Handbook of Powerful Spells Using Witches' Ladders and other Magical Knots*, London: New Burlington Press.

Bath, Jo (2002), *Dancing with the Devil: And Other True Tales of Northern Witchcraft*, Newcastle upon Tyne: Tyne Bridge Publishing.

Billock, Jennifer (2023), "The Un-Brie-Lievable History of Tyromancy", *Saveur*, www. saveur.com/culture/tyromancy-cheese-divination. Accessed 9 April 2024.

Binney, Ruth (2018), *Plant Lore and Legend: The Wisdom and Wonder of Plants and Flowers Revealed*, Hassocks: Rydon.

Breslaw, Philip (1792), *Breslaw's Last Legacy: or, The Conjuror Unmasked*, tenth edition, London: J Barker.

Bridget, Mrs (1790), *The Universal Fortune Teller: or, Mrs. Bridget's (Commonly Called* the Norwood Gipsy) Golden Treasury Explained, London: T. Sabine.

Burke, L. (1867), *The Illustrated Language of Flowers*, London: G. Routledge & Sons.

Carruthers, Miss (1879), *Flower Lore: The Teachings of Flowers, Historical, Legendary, Poetical & Symbolical*, London: George Bell & Sons.

Castelow, Ellen (no date), "Eve of St Agnes", *Historic UK*, www.historic-uk.com/CultureUK/Eve-of-St-Agnes. Accessed 2 February 2025.

Charsley, Simon (1988), "The Wedding Cake: History and Meanings", *Folklore*, 99:2, pp.232–41.

Clarke, Charles Cowden (1833), *Tales from Chaucer*, London: Effington Wilson.

Daniels, Cora Linn and C.M. Stevans (eds) (1971 [1903]a), *Encyclopaedia of Superstitions, Folklore, and the Occult Sciences of the World*, Volume 1, Chicago: Gale Research Company.

Daniels, Cora Linn and C.M. Stevans (eds) (1971 [1903]b), *Encyclopaedia of Superstitions, Folklore, and the Occult Sciences of the World*, Volume 2, Chicago: Gale Research Company.

Daniels, Cora Linn and C.M. Stevans (eds) (1971 [1903]c), *Encyclopaedia of Superstitions, Folklore, and the Occult Sciences of the World*, Volume 3, Chicago: Gale Research Company.

Davies, Owen (2007), *Popular Magic: Cunning-folk in English History*, London: Hambledon Continuum.

Davies, Owen (2017), "The World of Popular Magic", in Owen Davies (ed.), *The Oxford Illustrated History of Witchcraft and Magic*, Oxford: Oxford University Press, pp.167–94.

Day, Cyrus L. (1950), "Knots and Knot Lore", *Western Folklore*, 9:3, pp.229–56.

Dickson, T.W. (1927), "Magic: A Theme of Roman Elegy", *The Sewanee Review*, 35:4, pp.488–98.

Dietz, S. Theresa (2020), *The Complete Language of Flowers: A Definitive and Illustrated History*, New York: Wellfleet Press.

Dorsey, Lilith (2024), "Fabulous Folklore Presents … Tarot, Love Magic and Voodoo with Lilith Dorsey", *Fabulous Folklore Presents*, www.youtu.be/DYFd-jX-7DA?si=E_yJ9n-vMhAj9CeY. Accessed 11 December 2024.

Edmonds, J.M. (1912), *The Greek Bucolic Poets*, translated by J. M. Edmonds, Cambridge, MA: Harvard University Press.

Faraone, Christopher A. (1991), "Binding and Burying the Forces of Evil: The Defensive Use of 'Voodoo Dolls' in Ancient

Greece", *Classical Antiquity*, 10:2, pp.165–220.

Faraone, Christopher A. (2001), *Ancient Greek Love Magic*, Cambridge, MA: Harvard University Press.

Faraone, Christopher A. (2003), "When Spells Worked Magic", *Archaeology*, 56:2, pp.48–53.

Folkard, Richard (1884), *Plant lore, Legends, and Lyrics: Embracing the Myths, Traditions, Superstitions, and Folk-lore of the Plant Kingdom*, London: S. Low, Marston, Searle, and Rivington.

Francis, Francis (1874), *By Lake and River*, Frankfurt: Verlag.

García, Kristina (2022), "Possessed: The Salem Witch Trials", *Penn Today*, https://penntoday.upenn.edu/news/possessed-salem-witch-trials. Accessed 24 March 2025

Gary, Gemma (2022), *Wisht Waters: The Cult & Magic of Water*, London: Troy Books.

Gazur, Ben (2020), 'The Folklore of Bread', Ben Gazur, www.bengazur.com/post/the-folklore-of-bread. Accessed 4 March 2023.

Gomme, Alice Bertha (1898), *The Traditional Games of England, Scotland and Ireland*, Vol. 2, London: David Nutt.

Gray, Samantha (2015), *The Secret Language of Flowers*, London: CICO Books.

Guiley, Rosemary Ellen (2008), *The Encyclopedia of Witches, Witchcraft and Wicca*, third edition, New York: Facts On File.

Harrington, Christina Oakley (2020), *The Treadwell's Book of Plant Magic*, London: Treadwell's Books.

Hazlitt, William Carew (1905), *Faiths and Folklore: A Dictionary of National Beliefs, Superstitions and Popular Customs, Past and Current, with their Classical and Foreign Analogues*, Described and Illustrated, volume 1, London: Reeves & Turner.

Henderson, William (1879), *Notes on the Folk-lore of the Northern Counties of England and the Borders*, London: W. Satchell, Peyton and Co.

Herman, Eleanor (2011), *Sex with Kings: 500 Years of Adultery, Power, Rivalry, and Revenge*, New York: Barnes & Noble.

Herrick, Robert (1879 [1648]), *Hesperides: or the Works both Human and Divine*, Boston: Houghton, Osgood and Co.

Hole, Christina (1957), "Notes on Some Folklore Survivals in English Domestic Life", *Folklore*, 68:3, pp.411–19.

Hubbell, Diana (2022), "The Ancient Art of Kitchen Divination", *Atlas Obscura*, www.atlasobscura.com/articles/food-fortune-telling. Accessed 9 April 2024.

Ille-et-Vilaine Tourisme (no date), "La Roche-aux-Fées (Fairies' Rock)", *Ille-et-Vilaine Tourisme*, www.ille-et-vilaine-tourism.com/discover-ille-et-vilaine/the-loveliest-places/vitre/la-roche-aux-fees. Accessed 23 March 2024.

Inkwright, Fez (2020), *Folk Magic and Healing: An Unusual History of Everyday Plants*, London: Liminal 11 Press.

le Bas, John (1914), "Jersey Folklore Notes", *Folklore*, 25:2, pp.242–51.

Loomis, C. Grant (1956), "Italian Love Charms", *Western Folklore*, 15:2, p.134.

Lucas, Wendy (2018), "Damned by a Red Paragon Bodice: Witchcraft and the Power of Cloth and Clothing in Puritan Society", *Massachusetts Historical Review*, 20, pp.119–49.

Mac Coitir, Niall (2015), *Irish Trees: Myths, Legends & Folklore*, Cork: Collins Press.

Margaret, Annabel (2023), *The Green Witch's Guide to Herbal Magick: A Handbook of Green Hearthcraft and Plant-Based Spellcraft*, London: Quercus.

Mitchell, Laura (2013), "Love and the Longevity of Charms", *The Recipes Project*, https://recipes.hypotheses.org/1033. Accessed on 8 February 2020.

Monger, George (1994), "'To Marry in May': An Investigation of a Superstition", *Folklore*, 105, pp.104–8.

Opie, Iona and Moira Tatem (2005), *Oxford Dictionary of Superstitions*, Oxford: Oxford University Press.

Page, Sophie (2018), "Love in a Time of Demons: Magic and the Medieval Cosmos", in Sophie Page and Marina Wallace (eds), *Spellbound: Magic, Ritual and Witchcraft*, Oxford: Ashmolean Museum, pp.18–63.

Page, Sophie (2017a), *Magic in Medieval Manuscripts*, second edition, London: British Library Publishing.

Page, Sophie (2017b), "Medieval Magic", in Owen Davies (ed.), *The Oxford Illustrated History of Witchcraft and Magic*, Oxford: Oxford University Press, pp.29–64.

Phillips, George L. (1951), "Toss a Kiss to the Sweep for Luck", *The Journal of American Folklore*, 64:252, pp.191–96.

Plant Lore (2021), "Dandelion", Plant-Lore.com, www.plant-lore.com/dandelion. Accessed 1 April 2023.

Portelli, Alexandrine and Sam McKechnie (2015), *The Magpie & the Wardrobe: A Curiosity of Folklore, Magic and Spells*, London: Pavilion Books.

Rankine, David (2011), *The Grimoire of Arthur Gauntlet* [Sloane MS 3851], London: Avalonia.

Rider, Catherine (2012), *Magic and Religion in Medieval England*, London: Reaktion Books.

St Barbara Orthodox Church (2024), "Who Was Saint Barbara?", www.saintbarbarafw.org/who-was-saint-barbara. Accessed 2 February 2025.

Simina, Daniela (2023), *Where Fairies Meet: Parallels between Irish and Romanian Fairy Traditions*, Alresford: Moon Books.

Simpson, Jacqueline and Steve Roud (2007), *A Dictionary of English Folklore*, Oxford: Oxford University Press.

Sinclair, George (1814 [1685]), *Satan's Invisible World Discovered*, London: Printed for the Booksellers.

Stanmore, Tabitha (2024), *Cunning Folk: Life in the Era of Practical Magic*, London: Penguin Random House.

Stewart, Amy (2010), *Wicked Plants: The Weed that Killed Lincoln's Mother & Other Botanical Atrocities*, London: Timber Press.

StitchWitch (2019), "See a Pin and Pick it Up…", *Making of Magic*, https://makingofmagic.wordpress.com/2019/09/16/see-a-pin-and-pick-it-up. Accessed 24 February 2023.

Stott, Romie (2016), 'How Flower-Obsessed Victorians Encoded Messages in Bouquets', Atlas Obscura, www.atlasobscura.com/articles/how-flowerobsessed-victorians-encoded-messages-in-bouquets. Accessed 5 March 2022.

Strong, Isobel (1899), "The Teuila Fortune Cards", *The Puritan*, November, pp.217–27.

Taylor, Benjamin (1900), *Storyology: Essays in Folk-Lore, Sea-Lore, and Plant-Lore*, London: E. Stock.

Trevelyan, Marie (1909), *Folk-Lore and Folk-Stories of Wales*, London: Elliot Stock.

Valentine, Laura (1867), *The Language and Sentiment of Flowers*, London: Frederick Warne and Co.

Virgil (1994–2009), "Eclogue VIII", *The Eclogues*, written 37 BCE, https://classics.mit.edu/Virgil/eclogue.8.viii.html. Accessed 23 February 2025.

Waxman, Olivia B. (2016), "The Surprising Reasons Why Gingerbread Men Became a Holiday Classic", Time.com, https://time.com/4602913/gingerbread-men-history. Accessed 25 February 2025.

Wilde, Lady Jane Francesca (1888), "The Fatal Love-Charm", *Ancient Legends, Mystic Charms, and Superstitions of Ireland*, www.libraryireland.com/AncientLegendsSuperstitions/Contents.php. Accessed 13 February 2021.

References

1 Bath 2002: 13
2 Page 2017b: 61
3 Page 2018: 52
4 Page 2017b: 50
5 Stanmore 2024: 41
6 Stanmore 2024: 41
7 Rider 2012: 102
8 Taylor 1900: 65
9 Taylor 1900: 65
10 Taylor 1900: 65
11 Taylor 1900: 65
12 Sinclair 1814 [1685]: 143
13 Opie 2005: 349
14 Simpson 2007: 100
15 Sinclair 1814 [1685]: 142
16 Henderson 1879: 879: 91
17 Opie 2005: 120
18 Opie 2005: 121
19 Daniels 1971 [1903]c: 1494
20 St Barbara Orthodox Church 2024
21 Baker 2011 [1969]: 115
22 Baker 2011 [1969]: 140
23 Daniels 1971 [1903] b: 862
24 Mitchell 2013
25 Castelow, n.d.
26 Baker 2011 [1969]: 149
27 Castelow, n.d.
28 Daniels 1971 [1903] c: 1394
29 Baker 2011 [1969]: 64
30 Simina 2023
31 Baker 2011 [1969]: 105
32 Baker 2011 [1969]: 133
33 Opie 2005: 352
34 Henderson 1879: 175
35 Simpson 2007: 239
36 Mitchell 2013
37 Simpson 2007: 68
38 Inkwright 2020: 138
39 Simina 2022
40 Baker 2011 [1969]: 96
41 Simpson 2007: 383
42 Charsley 1988: 240
43 Daniels 1971[1903]a: 58
44 Henderson 1879: 35
45 Simpson 2007: 393
46 Francis 1874: 77
47 Henderson 1879: 230
48 Gary 2022: 60
49 Gary 2022: 61
50 Trevelyan 1909: 17
51 Loomis 1956: 134
52 Simpson 2007: 370
53 Dietz 2020: 215
54 Plant-Lore 2021
55 Daniels 1971 [1903] c: 1230
56 Dickson 1927: 488
57 Edmonds 1912: 24
58 Atsma 2000–2017
59 Henderson 1879: 176
60 Page 2017b: 62
61 Guiley 2008: 269
62 Herman 2011: 107
63 Stewart 2010: 106
64 Guiley 2008: 269
65 Guiley 2008: 269
66 Guiley 2008: 270
67 Daniels 1971 [1903] c: 1641
68 Burke 1867
69 Wilde 1888
70 Harrington 2020: 136
71 Daniels 1971 [1903] c: 1231
72 Henderson 1879: 11
73 Gazur 2020
74 Opie 2005: 39
75 Gazur 2020
76 Daniels 1971 [1903] c: 1394
77 Daniels 1971 [1903]c: 1393
78 Hubbell 2022
79 Billock 2023
80 Hubbell 2022
81 Opie 2005: 135
82 Opie 2005: 133
83 Hubbell 2022
84 Henderson 1879: 176
85 Henderson 1879: 174
86 Henderson 1879: 173
87 Henderson 1879: 173
88 Henderson 1879: 173
89 Opie 2005: 173
90 StitchWitch 2019
91 Henderson 1879: 175
92 Henderson 1879: 175
93 Opie 2005: 31
94 Henderson 1879: 35
95 Opie 2005: 310
96 Opie 2005: 311
97 Opie 2005: 311
98 Opie 2005: 311
99 StitchWitch 2019
100 Daniels 1971 [1903] a: 458
101 Opie 2005: 378
102 Opie 2005: 196
103 Simpson 2007: 325
104 le Bas 1914: 248
105 Opie 2005: 378
106 Daniels 1971 [1903] a: 80
107 Daniels 1971 [1903] a: 230
108 Daniels 1971 [1903] a: 459
109 Daniels 1971 [1903] a: 507
110 Opie 2005: 173
111 Daniels 1971 [1903] c: 1282

112 Daniels 1971 [1903]
c: 1283
113 Daniels 1971 [1903]
c: 1283
114 Day 1950: 229
115 Opie 2005: 222
116 Daniels 1971 [1903]
a: 465
117 Bartlett 2019: 6
118 Clarke 1833: 108
119 Simpson 2007: 241
120 Margaret 2023: 85
121 Dietz 2020: 33
122 Baker 2011 [1969]: 153
123 Harrington 2020: 123
124 Baker 2011 [1969]: 116
125 Baker 2011 [1969]: 152
126 Baker 2011 [1969]: 46
127 Baker 2011 [1969]: 130
128 Baker 2011 [1969]: 43
129 Baker 2011 [1969]: 11
130 Baker 2011 [1969]: 21
131 Baker 2011 [1969]: 130
132 Baker 2011 [1969]: 21
133 Opie 2005: 230
134 Baker 2011 [1969]: 43
135 Binney 2018: 131
136 Folkard 1884: 563
137 Baker 2011 [1969]: 71
138 Baker 2011 [1969]: 41
139 Binney 2018: 132
140 Opie 2005: 4
141 Baker 2011 [1969]: 8
142 Baker 2011 [1969]: 116
143 Opie 2005: 230
144 Folkard 1884: 506
145 Binney 2018: 132
146 Baker 2011 [1969]: 8
147 Daniels 1971 [1903]
b: 788
148 Opie 2005: 4
149 Binney 2018: 132
150 Baker 2011 [1969]: 76

151 Mac Coitir 2015
152 Mac Coitir 2015
153 Daniels 1971 [1903]:
b: 862
154 Stott 2016
155 Daniels 1971 [1903]
a: 465
156 Daniels 1971 [1903]
a: 467
157 Opie 2005: 91
158 Daniels 1971 [1903]
b: 675
159 Henderson 1879: 127
160 Hazlitt 1905: 96
161 Daniels 1971 [1903]
b: 666
162 Herrick 1879 [1648]:
190
163 Anonymous (1911
[1607]: 2)
164 Daniels 1971 [1903]
a: 90
165 Daniels 1971 [1903]
a: 89
166 Daniels 1971 [1903]
a: 83
167 Daniels 1971 [1903]
a: 440
168 Opie 2005: 154
169 Opie 2005: 154
170 Daniels 1971 [1903]
a: 440
171 Daniels 1971 [1903]
a: 441
172 Opie 2005: 151
173 Daniels 1971 [1903]
a: 441
174 Opie 2005: 150
175 Breslaw 1792: 44
176 Daniels 1971a: 221
177 Daniels 1971c: 1558
178 Daniels 1971b: 818
179 Daniels 1971a: 223
180 Breslaw 1792: 47

181 Daniels 1971a: 228
182 Breslaw 1792: 46
183 Breslaw 1792: 46
184 Daniels 1971a: 228
185 Daniels 1971a: 229
186 Daniels 1971a: 228
187 Breslaw 1792: 48
188 1792: 47
189 Breslaw 1792: 48
190 Breslaw 1792: 51
191 Bridget 1790: 46
192 Bridget 1790: 46
193 Bridget 1790: 46
194 Bridget 1790: 43
195 Bridget 1790: 43
196 Bridget 1790: 44
197 Daniels 1971a: 228
198 Bridget 1790: 45
199 Daniels 1971a: 225
1792: 46
200 Breslaw 1792: 46
201 Daniels 1971a: 225
202 Breslaw 1792: 48
203 Breslaw 1792: 47
204 Breslaw 1792: 46
205 Daniels 1971a: 228
206 Daniels 1971a: 228
207 Daniels 1971a: 229
208 Breslaw 1792: 49
209 Breslaw 1792: 47
210 Breslaw 1792: 51
211 Bridget 1790: 45
212 Bridget 1790: 45
213 Faraone 1991: 175
214 Faraone 1991: 189
215 Faraone 1991: 190
216 Virgil 1994–2009
217 Dickson 1927: 488
218 collections.louvre.
fr/ en/ark:/53355/
cl010011467
219 Faraone 2003: 52
220 Faraone 2003: 51

221 Faraone 2003: 51

222 Faraone 2003: 53

223 Stanmore 2024: 50

224 Brown, quoted in García 2022

225 Lucas 2018: 120

226 Lucas 2018: 135

227 Lucas 2018: 136

228 Davies 2007: x

229 Rankine 2011: 150

230 Rankine 2011: 151

231 Davies 2017: 177

232 Waxman 2016

233 Levin quoted in Waxman 2016

234 Waxman 2016

235 Dietz 2020: 191

236 Bailliot 2015: 96

237 Simpson 2007: 283

238 Gomme 1898: 41

239 Simpson 2007: 283

240 American Folklore Society 1895: 251

241 Daniels 1971 [1903] c: 1285

242 Daniels 1971 [1903] c: 1286

243 Daniels 1971 [1903] c: 1471

244 Daniels 1971 [1903] c: 1476

245 Daniels 1971 [1903] c: 1477

246 Daniels 1971 [1903] c: 1478

247 Dorsey 2024

248 Barbier 2023

249 Strong 1899: 217

250 Faraone 2001: 110

251 Ille-et-Vilaine Tourisme, n.d.

252 Baker 2011 [1969]: 105

253 Baker 2011 [1969]: 115

254 Mac Coitir 2015

255 Burke 1867: 11

256 Baker 2011 [1969]: 141

257 Carruthers 1879: 17

258 Gray 2015: 103

259 Portelli 2015

260 Simpson 2007: 382

261 Henderson 1879: 33

262 Simpson 2007: 382

263 Monger 1994: 107

264 Monger 1994: 104

265 Portelli 2015

266 Portelli 2015

267 Simpson 2007: 60

268 Leach, quoted in Phillips 1951: 191

269 Simpson 2007: 384

270 Henderson 1879: 34

271 Wakeman, quoted in The Journal of American Folklore 1892: 238

272 Simpson 2007: 384

273 Hole 1957: 418

274 Hole 1957: 418

275 Simpson 2007: 325

276 Opie 2005: 351

277 Opie 2005: 351

278 Portelli 2015

279 Simpson 2007: 384

280 Simpson 2007: 384

281 Simpson 2007: 28

282 Henderson 1879: 34

283 Simpson 2007: 384

284 Opie 2005: 197

285 Opie 2005: 152

286 Dietz 2020: 40

287 Dietz 2020: 191

288 Harrington 2020: 100

289 Dietz 2020: 12

290 Baker 2011: 128

291 Faraone 2001: 70

292 Faraone 2001: 71

293 Faraone 2001: 72

294 Dietz 2020: 153

295 Dietz 2020: 66

296 Baker 2011 [1969]: 71

297 Baker 2011 [1969]: 72

298 Dietz 2020: 126

299 Valentine 1867: 82

300 Dietz 2020: 154

301 Dietz 2020: 145

302 Baker 2011 [1969]: 104

303 Dietz 2020: 61

304 Dietz 2020: 56

305 Dietz 2020: 191

306 Baker 2011 [1969]: 153

307 Burke 1867: 61

308 Baker 2011 [1969]: 96

309 Baker 2011 [1969]: 9

310 Baker 2011 [1969]: 101

311 Baker 2011 [1969]: 149

312 Baker 2011 [1969]: 37

313 Dietz 2020: 20

314 Dietz 2020: 201

315 Baker 2011 [1969]: 43

316 Harrington 2020: 95

317 Folkard 1884: 505

318 Dietz 2020: 151

319 Daniels 1971 [1903] a: 440

320 Stanmore 2024: 55

321 Binney 2018: 27

322 Stanmore 2024: 54

323 Stanmore 2024: 56

324 Stanmore 2024: 54

325 Davies 2007: 101

326 Dietz 2020: 52

327 Dietz 2020: 38

328 Davies 2007: 102

329 Davies 2007: 102

ABOUT THE AUTHOR

Icy Sedgwick is the host of the Fabulous Folklore podcast, investigating the strange and often bizarre world of European folklore (with a focus on the British Isles). She's particularly fascinated by the appearance of folklore in popular culture, but also the ways in which folklore preserves information in an easily transmissible format. Love magic and love divination became specialist subjects by accident after she noticed it cropping up in the most unlikely places – the bread section of this book is a good example!

In case she tires of all that folklore research, former ghost hunter Icy also writes Gothic horror fiction and holds a PhD in Film Studies; in her thesis, she examined the representation of haunted houses in contemporary Hollywood cinema. She was born and raised in the north east of England, where she lives and haunts the libraries in Newcastle. Like any good folklorist, she has a horseshoe over her door, and she doesn't stray too close to mushroom rings …

ACKNOWLEGEMENTS

I want to thank Fiona Robertson for taking a chance on this book; I'm forever grateful that she saw the potential for a deep dive into a pet topic of mine. I also thank everyone at Watkins who had a hand in bringing this book to life – you're all magical people.

Next, I want to thank my family, since they had to put up with me randomly mentioning a love ritual or divination at often the most inopportune times, and they've always been very supportive of my desire to preserve these folk practices for the future. Likewise, thank you to my friends, who watched me try these practices, and listened to me complaining when they didn't work!

I also want to thank the Fabulous Folklore listeners who encouraged me to research this topic further, and my Patrons for supporting the podcast so I can do this work. You're all wonderful!

Finally, I thank all of the folklorists, writers and researchers who preserved this information, for whatever reason they chose to do so. They made my job in collating this information so much easier – and more joyful – and I hope to pass on some of that joy to you, dear reader!

INDEX